MAURICE TORNAY

An inspiring tale but very prudent when
you try to imitate
Happy Christmas 1993

Francis
CRIC

Claire Marquis-Oggier
Jacques Darbellay

MAURICE TORNAY

A man seized by God

ST PAULS

Original title: *Le Bienheureux Maurice Tornay, un homme séduit par Dieu*

Translation by Sr Edmond Veronica RA

Cover: Blessed Maurice Tornay by Klaus and Barbara Kegellmann, 1993
(The portrait for the Beatification).

ST PAULS
Middlegreen, Slough SL3 6BT, United Kingdom
Moyglare Road, Maynooth, Co. Kildare, Ireland

© Angelin-Maurice Lovey CRB 1993

ISBN 085439 446 X

Printed in the EEC by Loader Jackson Printers, Arlesey

ST PAULS is an activity of the priests and brothers of the Society of St Paul
who proclaim the Gospel through the media of social communication

CONTENTS

Preface

Why should there be another new book on Father Maurice Tornay when there are already several which are very well written? Certainly, *A Martyr in Tibet*, by R. Loup, *Land of Iron and Sky of Bronze* by M. Zermatten or again, *An X-ray of a Soul*, which contains the presentation of the Cause and the advocate's speech, each have their particular merit and played a positive role in advancing the Cause. However, none of these works benefitted either from all the documents contained in the *Positio*, or from those issued later such as the preambles of the theologian-consultors, and more especially the decree of His Holiness John Paul II which conferred the title of "Martyr of the Faith", on the Servant of God.

This decree, promulgated in Rome, 11 July 1992, ended the long preliminary procedure and opened up the path for the beatification of Father Maurice Tornay. Thus a new biography seemed necessary where, for the first time, the title "Blessed" might be added to Maurice Tornay's name.

Mr Jacques Darbellay and Mrs Claire Marquis-Oggier, the authors of this biography, entitled *Maurice Tornay, a man seized by God*, were able to use all the documents connected with the Cause.

I am amazed at the synthesis, so concise and so complete, that they have produced, often using the correspondence of Blessed Maurice and pointing out his dominant trait: the constant desire for holiness, both during his childhood, then as a student and, very markedly, from the time of his entry with the Canons Regular of Mont-Joux, in the Great St Bernard Abbey. This desire grew greatly during the difficult and sometimes dramatic circumstances of his missionary life in China and Tibet.

7

I cannot thank these two authors sufficiently for their devotedness and their complete disinterestedness. They accepted to put aside other plans and gave up part of their summer vacation so that the original version, and the many translations into different foreign languages, would be ready in time for the beatification. May God and his faithful servant repay them fully!

Finally, let us hope that this work may give all the readers, particularly young people, an ardent desire to imitate the newly beatified in his incessant search for holiness and his devotedness to others even to the shedding of their blood, should this prove necessary.

Jesus has said: "Blessed are those who hunger and thirst for justice, or holiness, for they will be filled" Matthew 5:6.

* * *

If this work appears today it is also, and above all, because many people have worked for the past forty years to bring about the successful issue of the Cause of Father Maurice Tornay. Many did it voluntarily out of pure love, or to show their gratitude to our glorious martyr.

It is quite impossible to mention each person as inevitably someone or other will be missed out. However, I must name several to whom we owe a special debt of gratitude. Mgr Nestor Adam, Bishop of Sion; Abbe Henri Depommier, Defender of the Faith; Canon Charles Giroud, the first Vice-Postulator; Canon Pierre-Marie Kelly, who through the magazine *The Great St Bernard,Tibet* made the Servant of God known to many people. He also saw to the publication of *A Martyr in Tibet*, by Robert Loup, which later was translated into German, Italian, English and Spanish; to the Canons of the Lateran: Don Giorgio Scatena and Emilio Dunoyer, successively postulators; to the lawyers Carlo Snider and Andrea Ambrosi; to the writer Maurice Zermatten author of *Land of Iron and Sky of Bronze,* or the Passion of Father Maurice Tornay; to the Congregation for the Causes of Saints, during the forty years of the proceedings: notably to Cardinal Edouard Gagnon, Ponent of the Cause; Reverend Father Ambroise Eszer OP. General Postulator; Mgr Antonio Patti, Promotor of the Faith; the theologian-consulters and so many others, often unknown to the undersigned who, during the whole procedure for the Cause played a discreet but efficacious role.

Very warm and particularly grateful thanks to all those who by their gifts, both large and small, gave material support to the cause of the one who may now be called Blessed.

Special thanks also to Sr Edmond Veronica RA responsible for the translation of this text from French into English and to St Pauls who produced the English edition.

Last but not least, an immense and very respectful thanks to His Holiness Pope John Paul II, who deigned to ratify and crown all these efforts by giving the title of *Martyr of the Faith*, to the Servant of God Maurice Tornay and by raising him to the honours of the altar. May God preserve him for the Church for a long time, give him health, strength and courage that he may continue to feed the flock entrusted to him with the wisdom and zeal that have characterised the whole of his pontificate.

+Angelin-Maurice Lovey CRB
Abbé Provost emeritus of the Great St Bernard Abbey
Vice-Postulator

Why Tibet?

Maurice Tornay, canon of the Great St Bernard Order, died
in an ambush on the border between Yunnan and Tibet.
Everyone in Valais has heard something of his story. Many
Christians both in Switzerland and far beyond, interested in
the missions, wanted to know more about him, especially
since they learnt that a process for his Beatification was
initiated in 1953. They also learnt that, during the summer
of 1992, the Holy Father had promulgated the decree con-
cerning "the martyrdom of the Servant of God, Maurice
Tornay, professed priest of the Congregation of Saints
Nicholas and Bernard of Mont-Joux, killed in 1949, out of
hatred for the Faith". This decree was published in Rome,
11 July 1992.

Two remarkable works *The Martyr in Tibet* by Robert
Loup, second edition 1953, and *Land of Iron and Sky of
Bronze* by Maurice Zermatten, 1988, have already made
known to a large public the blazing trail traced by the child
of La Rosiere, desirous of the absolute, who, aged twenty-
five, went to the ends of the earth to serve the poor and
exploited population until his final supreme sacrifice.

The beatification of the Servant of God calls us to pose
once again the essential questions. Who was Maurice
Tornay? How did he spend his childhood and in what kind
of family? Where and how did he pass the decisive years of
his early youth? What kind of student was he and what kind
of seminarian? Where did the idea of becoming a missionary in Tibet spring from? Why choose just this region of
the world which is one of the most inaccessible, the fur-
thest from all that might be known to him, the most troubled also during the years of civil war in China. Later came
the victory of the communist troops over the Nationalist

army which the Allies had supported. This victory marked the end of Tibetan independence, proclaimed in 1912. In Yunnan where the missionaries were working, the victory was foreshadowed by upheavals, famine, attacks by brigands, great insecurity and many expulsions. Yet in all these difficulties Fr Tornay risked his life to remain true to his commitment.

How does a vocation to holiness in the 20th century come to life, how is it strengthened and finally realised? It is true, youth is always drawn by great ideals, and feels called to great sacrifices and to generosity. At certain moments the attraction of the total gift of self towards the absolute becomes almost impelling. But the spirit of the times asks itself: Is this a vocation or a temptation? The desire to go beyond oneself, to tend to perfection, surely contains a certain measure of pride. The voice of the world, social pressure, even the influence of education, agrees with popular wisdom which clips the wings of great ambitions, suggests an "accommodating virtue" and signals the middle way as being the most desirable for the individual and the most reassuring for society.

To present Maurice Tornay at the moment of his beatification, more than forty years after his death, means to take into account the questions that the readers of the year 2000 will ask. They will certainly not ask them in quite the same way as the deeply religious communities of the years 1920-1950 would have asked.

The life of the one whom the official documents name as the Servant of God, seems very near to us chronologically (1910-1949) and yet very remote because of the time he spent apparently outside our world: five years in the Great St Bernard Abbey, followed by thirteen years in the Chinese area of Yunnan on the southern borders of fabled Tibet.

Until it was halfway over, the 20th century appeared to be turned towards a past already frozen in unchanging history. In contrast, the last three or four decades give us the impression that everything has been set in motion and is rushing into the future to seek an unattainable anchorage as soon as possible. This feeling is increased by the kind of bottle-neck phenomenon which is drawing us quickly to the end of the century and the millennium. We seem to be moving ahead, but on the same spot, or we seem to be on board a ship tacking on the high seas, seeking a port seen in a mirage. We seem to be in a rocket whizzing in orbit whose landing is indefinitely postponed. We would like to reach and remain at the next stop which is always slipping away like the prey running from the arrow of Zenon of Elea.

On the contrary, from his youth Maurice Tornay wanted to set off for distant lands. Although the land where he lived was not affected by the call of the sea winds, he himself wanted to set sail to the ends of the earth and go beyond his own limits. What was his driving force? If we could answer this question fully, we would have clarified part of the secret of his existence, and lifted a corner of the veil which hides him from our reasoning. As with all the great adventurers of God, we must begin by sharing in his spiritual journey in some way so that we may understand it.

In certain aspects, Maurice Tornay can appear not to share the preoccupations or the feeling of our time. We need to show this is not so, that his faith, his care of others, the place he gave as a youth to contacts with those around him, all give to the rigours of his project an actuality that goes beyond prevailing fads and modes and resists the erosion of time.

As we shall see, his was a personality that broke through the norms and conventions of an epoch. Formalism does not interest him. He was never limited by religious conformism even during his early childhood which was lively and pious. Others, especially those near him, would help him to achieve his great passion, the desire to give himself entirely to God. He could never have realised those dreams without them. It is striking to note the place affectivity had in his life, in his direct and cordial sharing, and in a kind of spiritual friendship with others which

13

characterised his apostolate with his friends, when he entered college at fifteen.

It is important to notice how the behaviour of this young shepherd boy, this student, strikes all who knew him or guided him. He had a strong character with a wide range of qualities and virtues, with faults as well and these, over the years became unified and harmonised, thanks to his immense desire to prepare himself worthily for the great cause without denying the originality of his nature.

This mischievous and yet serious child, stubborn and intelligent, was attentive to a call he heard very early on, re-discovered as a student and seminarian and fulfilled as the parish priest at Yerkalo. The unity and fidelity of this life willingly offered, both impresses and challenges us.

La Rosiere: his roots

The short life of Maurice Tornay, 1910–1949, is divided into three more or less equal stages: his childhood at La Rosiere which lasted till he was fifteen; a period of eleven years of study at the Abbey of St Maurice and then in the Great St Bernard Hospice; finally his thirteen years of active life as a missionary in Yunnan on the south-east border of Tibet.

La Rosiere is a small village with a dozen homesteads clinging to a spur above Orsieres on the right bank of the Dranse about 1200m above sea-level. The houses are built of local stone, there are stables, haylofts, storage barns for the sheaves awaiting winter threshing and a cheese-making dairy. There is a bakery on the ground floor of the little school and a gleaming white chapel dedicated to St Anne. Nothing has changed in the village since the beginning of the century except that the roads and alleys are now tarred, the fountain has been moved and there is a simple green near the entrance to the village. Two of the barns have been adapted as homes and the chapel has been tastefully restored. There is nothing to attract the occasional passer-by in the old alley-ways of La Rosiere but a certain simplicity which suits the mountain life-style.

The carefully tended and fertile gardens and the surrounding fields appear to be in better shape than the dwellings, but this is always so in these little alpine villages where survival depends on the land. For us, following the traces of Maurice Tornay who was born here in 1910, everything seems full of meaning and mystery. His birthplace, one in a row of houses, is hidden, confined and dark, looking westwards towards the steep slopes of Mt Catogne which blocks the horizon.

All the opinions about the Tornay family are very similar. They were seen as honourable, as Christians who were faithful to their religious practices and who liked to pray together. They were extremely hard-working but not at all well-off in spite of possessing several plots of land, some meadows for spring and summer grazing at Cretes, and a vineyard in Fully. "Our parents were very poor", noted one of Maurice's brothers. This was quite true but this poverty was normal in La Rosiere. Maurice's father, John, traded in live-stock, and is still called the "go between" by those who knew him. His mother, Faustine Rossier, practised a hidden charity which she taught to her children. "Mama could never see anyone else suffering without suffering herself", commented her son Louis. It became clear from the different testimonies that she fulfilled the task of mother of a large family to perfection, with a sensitive and communicative charisma. Maurice revered her as a saint. He was the seventh of eight children, three boys and five girls of whom one died in infancy. Like all the children of these large peasant families they had tasks which suited their strength, in the house, in the fields, with the animals, up in the meadows from June to September, or in the vineyard, according to the needs of the seasons.

Maurice, "a little spoiled because he was the last boy," say his elders, did his share of work all the same. From the time he was twelve he was capable of anything including milking and cheese-making. He preferred dealing with the animals. Robert Loup, who asked about him in La Rosiere immediately after his death, noted this incident. The summer of 1922 was extremely wet, so life at the high meadow was very hard. The chief shepherd and the servants went away, so his father asked him, "Maurice, would you like to go up there"? "Yes of course." "But you are too young."

Maurice answered, "Not at all! Don't worry about me. We can't leave the meadow at mid-summer; besides I want to see Violette fight." He was allowed to go and proved himself worthy of the confidence placed in him.

It must be said that young Maurice had a strong

character. Here is a list, in no particular order, of some of the things said about him as a child: he was courageous, head-strong, proud, bossy, unafraid of disputing with adults, had a lively mind, was pugnacious. He told the truth without fear of making enemies, and was pious. In fact his teacher said of him at fourteen, "He was the most pious boy in the class." Quick and fiery he never showed resentment. "We would make up and perhaps shed a few tears together", said one of his sisters, about their quarrels. "He was afraid of nothing and nobody and would readily stay alone in the upper meadows even at night or would return to the village in the dark, going alone through the gloomy forest. He was hard on himself, had great endurance and an extraordinary will", said one of his neighbours three years younger than he. He was artful, explosive, impetuous, fiery and persevering.

His sister Anna, two years younger than he, says of him, "He was well ahead of the boys of his own age which made him proud and he even attempted to teach his elder brothers and sisters. He was very rough and sometimes hit me. He was always sorry and apologised afterwards only to begin again a short time later."

Such was the young scamp of La Rosiere as seen by those who spent that part of his life on the mountain with him. What would he make of that assortment of striking qualities and unpleasant failings, in college, in the noviciate and on the missions?

His brother Louis tells the following story about him: "Maurice must have been about four because he could speak easily. We were both in the living room with Mama and an aunt. I was playing my game and he was occupied with his. He was placing tiny objects round the hearth made of the strong green stone of the district. Suddenly he stopped and went to Mama and asked, "Mama, is it better to be a priest or the head teacher?" Mama and my aunt began to laugh and Mama answered, "Oh, it is better to become a priest." Later on when we confided in each other he told me it was from that moment he knew what his vocation was.

Listen once more to his sister, Anna: "I was studying my catechism which had inside it a holy picture of St Agnes, virgin and martyr. I told Mama I wanted to be a virgin. Mama explained that so I was. "And Maurice?" "Yes, he is also." We were both very content with that but we also wanted to know how to become martyrs. Mama explained that we should love God above all things and be ready to die rather than offend him. Maurice commented, "That's quite true. You will see, I shall be a martyr."

There you see him when he was young. Each one has his own destiny. It seems clear that for Maurice there were already several gold nuggets gleaming among the dross. However he, like many great souls, in the search for unity, balance and the path to perfection would have to face many struggles and difficulties. A little later on we will see how he tried to calm his turbulent nature and to conquer himself by renunciation, sacrifice and suffering.

One might conclude from looking at his childhood that everything had been easy for him in his family life, in the village and at school. He was gifted and had acquired the indispensible skills needed to fit in harmoniously with the many hard tasks in which all shared. Of course the adults took on the heaviest work but Maurice's role was important if we consider the time and care needed in looking after the goats, sheep and calves, all large animals. Think also of the precarious life at Cretes almost two hours above La Rosiere, where there were two huts, one at 1800m and the other at 2000m. There, with makeshift means he had to keep house without running water or electricity. He ate bread, potatoes and cheese brought from the valley on a donkey at the end of May or the beginning of June when they were first installed. After milking he had his daily drink. Anything extra needed was brought when he received an occasional visit.

The heavier work of the village, hay-making, harvesting, autumnal labours and care of the vineyard at Fully needed the strength of the strongest adults down in the valley. The young people worked up on the mountain and with thoughtfulness and generosity did all they could to finish the tasks, getting up at dawn and going to bed late at night. They thus lightened the load weighing on their parents and older people, who were needed elsewhere. This was their daily adventure, in the freezing dawn, in rain or snow but also on beautiful sunny days, marooned in a kind of island on top of the world, called by everyone "our beloved Cretes" even when these days were merely a memory. They felt they belonged there, that they were masters over a corner of the earth and as needs arose they invented all that helped this "microcosm" to exist and to provide precious provisions like cheese and butter, which they stored in a cool place. What an experience of life for those boys and girls from ten to sixteen and how proud their parents must have been to be able to count on them. Yet how their mother must have worried knowing they were alone on the mountain heights during certain stormy nights!

An ordinary childhood perhaps, in a hard and sometimes inhuman world where good and evil were locked in combat with people and even history itself at stake.

A depressing vision, perhaps even manichean, but it is hard not to feel how harsh and relentless the work was, all the year round, just to gain enough to live on. It seemed as if the pressure never eased off. There was no time, once the work was finished, to celebrate the joy of being together, free and happy. Did not this land which provided their livelihood demand too much in return? Did not those who served it so assiduously become like slaves? Was it a kind-hearted mother or a possessive and ungrateful stepmother? Did it not risk seizing hold of the hearts and feelings of those who worked so hard, like a jealous mistress who brooks no rivals? The young Maurice was caught up in this climate of incessant labour and worked untiringly, but he never gave the impression of being completely shut in by it. He seemed to be occupied with questions that he did not then express but which would appear later in his letters from afar, when he saw those dear to him were always as closely bound as ever to the ancestral soil.

One should be watchful for little signs. His brother Louis, seven years his elder, noted, "When Maurice was quite young he was both a dreamer and an observer. He would sit quite still on the same spot gazing into space, yet observing everything, his face already marked by sadness. Mama was anxious when she saw her child seated like that and remaining so still."

We have already seen that he was very active, joyful and mischievous, quick to defend his rights and those of his family. But he did not always rush into action immediately. His sister Anna who later became a religious with the Sisters of Charity at La Roche-sur-Foron remembers this fact: "During the holidays he often slipped away alone. I was close to him but he did not want me with him on these occasions because I would be in the way. He would usually go to some quiet spot in the forest. One day, as I passed near, I saw that he was meditating. When he returned from these times of prayer he sometimes confided his resolutions to me. Once he told me he had resolved to go regularly every week to confession. We were up on Les Cretes at that time and every Saturday he went down to Orsieres in time for Sunday morning when he went to confession before Mass."

La Rosiere forms part of the Orsieres parish, a town of some two thousand inhabitants, situated where the River Dranse of Entremont and that of Ferret meet. Orsieres is about an hour on foot from La Rosiere but two and a half from Cretes. It was in the church dedicated to St Nicholas of Myre that Maurice was baptised, confirmed and received his First Communion at the age of twelve. On that occasion Anna whispered to one of her sisters, "Maurice has really changed and has become very kind!"

He went to Orsieres for his last year at school as did all the better pupils, to follow an advanced class there. He walked there and back morning and evening whatever the weather, not at all unusual in those days. It was both an opportunity and an honour to be selected for this class.

Since he was anxious to continue his studies, for he

desired to become a priest among the Canons of the Great St Bernard, he went to the Hospice with his parents before he went to Secondary School. His childhood ends with a step that committed not only his own future and that of his family, but also that of the great family of the Religious of St Bernard he wished to enter one day.

What dreams filled this adolescent as he climbed the mountain paths in the summer of 1925? What promise did he make, when he came to confide the vocation he had felt for the last eleven years, to the Abbot of the Congregation? We know nothing. Even to the sister he trusted he never spoke of this. It remains a secret between God and himself.

The shepherd boy at the Royal Abbey

In October 1925, Maurice Tornay entered the College of the Abbey of St Maurice. He was fifteen and would be a boarder for the next six years. Secondary studies usually began about the age of thirteen or fourteen but because of the hard work the family had to do, he was kept at home as long as possible. Since he had followed the advanced class in Orsieres the previous year, it was thought that he would not be too far behind in the studies at St Maurice. This proved true in certain subjects but he had never learnt Latin and as this was taught for seven hours a week in the first year of college, Maurice had to work in a beginners' class with students one or two years younger than himself.

We already know this boy from the mountains, we know his character, his plans and the special world he would leave behind for nine months of the year. Yet it would never really be far from his mind since it was part of his roots and for many years to come it would fill his inner world. On the one hand was his family, the land, the animals and Cretes, and on the other, his faith and his vocation. This move to boarding school life and college must have been a tremendous and sudden uprooting!

What we have learnt of him up to this point comes from the testimonies given during the process presided over by the Bishop of Sion from 1953 till 1963. We have scarcely heard his own voice. From now on, all that touches him intimately is revealed to us in his letters. A few lines from the first letter from the college to his parents and family set the tone. "Here we are almost at the end of this beautiful month of October, filled with delights for the student. It is no exaggeration when I tell you that I am well and that I like it here. I find college life the happiest and loveliest to be found in this world of sacrifices." He would never think of complaining or discussing his difficulties for his life at college was easy compared with that of his family working on the mountain-side. It is they who made the sacrifice having to do without his help and by offering him the chance to study.

As for himself, he had decided to offer his life to God; he did not know where or how this would be achieved but he realised that his studies were part of the preparation for it. We are struck by his insistence in asking his friends to help him by offering their sorrows, thoughts and joys. To become a saint, the great project which was always his aim, great strength of character was needed to remain firm on every occasion and to go even as far as real heroism. Not having the virtues, acquired in bitter combat, weaknesses can be offered, giving what one is and leaving to God the job of arranging it all. This vision of things can be seen in all his correspondance. He wrote one hundred and sixty-six letters covering three hundred and forty typewritten sheets. The resemblance to the "Little Way" of St Thérèse of the Child Jesus is striking, less in the expression than in the spiritual attitude. It is clearer in the letters written from St Maurice and from the Great St Bernard Abbey than in those from Yunnan. This is a mere intuition that might enlighten us, so it is noted in passing as it might be helpful.

At that time many people in the villages and at St Maurice Abbey would have been speaking about the little Carmelite of Lisieux who died aged twenty-four in 1897. Many articles about her would have appeared in the parish newsletters. Her canonisation, 17 May 1925, four months before Maurice went to college, drew such an immense crowd to Rome that the Pope himself was astonished, he who considered St Thérèse as the star of his pontificate. Two years later she was named "Patron of the Missions," although she had entered Carmel at fifteen and never went out again. We have no intention of comparing Maurice's vocation with that of Thérèse. Each saint has his or her own way. Holiness consists in discovering one's call and then in giving oneself to this without reserve. By temperament Maurice was inclined to action, including action on himself, which is the most demanding of all, and very early on he realised this would demand heroism of him. However the example of St Thérèse enlightened him and supported him in his choices and in his daily life but he made no specific allusions to her in his letters. A student who was his classmate for three years gave this interesting indication in his testimony: "He led us to do good. He took about a dozen of us in our spare time in the afternoon, to meditate for a short while in the chapel... He often read from St Francis of Sales and from St Thérèse of the Child Jesus."

As, in addition to his letters, we get to know the writings of the Servant of God which cover one hundred and twenty-five pages, we discover a document which makes our hypothesis tenable not only of a spiritual closeness with Thérèse of Lisieux, but also of a familiarity with her writings and a deep trust in her. Here is a prayer which has no date but was probably composed by Maurice in college:

"Be mindful, O Blessed Thérèse, of our miseries and of the hope your promises have given us. You promised to spend your heaven doing good on earth, and that your mission would last as long as the world. You often said that it is important to pray for priests so that Jesus may be loved. I am going to become a priest. Will you refuse me the help you have given to so many others for mere worldly advantages as I seek to reach my goal? Obtain humility for me, a trusting humility."

But we must not go too far ahead. Maurice still needed a lot of smoothing and grooming when he was in the boarding school. In general teachers and warders recognised him as "an excellent subject", but then they would quickly add, "but as twisted as an Orserens." A doctor who saw him frequently at the conferences of St Vincent de Paul said, "One could make a doctor of him in a year, but then what determination he has!" Several witnesses speak of his authoritarian temperament: "a leader who

24

brought his followers round to his point of view and whom he formed into a group." "When he was studying classics, just before we were supposed to have a French examination, Tornay told me to fold my arms and before the professor came in he turned to the class and threatened, 'If anyone picks up his pencil or pen I will snap it in half!'" On another occasion, as several witnesss testify, he was dissatisfied with the teacher who edited the review, *Echoes of St Maurice* and persuaded his classmates to return their copies. They all did so that same evening. The teacher on duty, who had been told about it, discussed the matter with Tornay who went back on his decision so all was settled without further consequences. Young Maurice had his vision of things and charged ahead to reach them. But afterwards he was willing to listen to other points of view and once convinced of his faults would give in even if his pride was hurt.

These are extreme examples but there is nothing in them that needs to be retracted. His difficulties, his impetuosity, even his excesses serve to show up his efforts, his fight against himself and his endeavour to lift himself up "towards the goal of perfection", according to Mgr Adam's expression. Monsignor was his Superior in 1931 and then became Abbot of the Congregation of the Great St Bernard in 1939 and Bishop of Sion in 1952.

There are also very encouraging accounts about his life at college. He studied perseveringly in college and obtained excellent results. He had a very good memory and a remarkable and lively intelligence which could quickly seize on the difficulties. His teachers, when questioned by Robert Loup just after Maurice's death, agree with the following description: "A very hard-working, intelligent student, genuinely joyful and of fervent piety. He always gained the first place which did not in any way diminish his simplicity. His was a determined vocation, such as is found among the highland people of Valais, of whom it can be said with almost complete certainty, 'They are people who never look back'."

All the same he was tempted to change his path. His facility in studies, his dominance over his companions, his debating skills and his ability to defend his opinions held out bright prospects should he choose to become a barrister. He would then form part of the political scene of Valais, even of Switzerland itself, and he would earn plenty of money and thus be able to help his family. His brother Louis states that during his first years in college this idea proved a "violent temptation" for Maurice who never spoke of it in his letters. He seems never to have mentioned it to anyone except Louis in whom he often confided when he was a student.

Some qualities are repeatedly cited and are doubtless the dominant characteristics of his moral portrait: he was said to be open, pure and pious. He might be a tease, a practical joker, inclined to be aggressive, pugnacious and obstinate but he never compromised with the truth. Mgr Angelin Lovey, the distinguished Abbot, who himself came from the Orsieres district, knew him better than anyone. He was his classmate for six years and his brother in the Great St Bernard Abbey from 1931 to 1936, and on the same mission from 1939 to 1949; he does not hesitate to say, "He was a model of purity... he loved philosophy and discussing philosophical questions, he was poetic and contemplative." The authors he most often quoted are Moliere, Bloy, Peguy, Psichari, Claudel and Bernanos, with St Augustine, Suarez, Maritain and Billot on theological and spiritual matters.

But it is time we heard Maurice speak for himself to show us a side of his nature still unknown to us, his great gift of communicating. Generally, mountain people are reserved, timid and introvert.

Young Maurice, whether by a natural disposition or by determination, conquered this reserve and discussed with his family the question that concerned him more and more: his religious commitment and his search for perfection. He felt the need to share this and to draw his friends after him in the same spiritual search. Here is a selection of extracts from his letters that set the tone.

On 12 December 1927, in a letter to his brother Louis, he wrote: "In all my difficulties and troubles I try to find something fresh for my spirit and something salutary for my soul. That is the way to reach the goal and is it not also the way to gain the eternal palm?"

On 4 January 1929, he wrote to his parents and family as if he were addressing God: "We are nothing, not even a grain of sand beside the ocean but from our extreme poverty, humbly and with faith and love we ask You to re-establish in heaven this family which, with so many others, adorned the little village of La Rosiere."

On 4 May 1930, he wrote to Louis: "For us Christians, after baptism there are not two lives but only one. We climb the ladder of love as in a dream in this world; after death we will awaken on the same ladder, but in the dazzling reality. You stretch out your hand to me here below. I will stretch out mine to you when I arrive in heaven." This outstretched hand signifies the fact that Louis often answered requests from the penniless student when he needed to purchase some little trifle or, above all, to buy books. Maurice promised to repay him from heaven because, although he was seven years younger, he sensed that he would reach the goal first.

On 5 October 1930, he wrote to one of his sisters who had stayed at home to manage the homestead and to help her parents: "I enjoyed myself looking into your soul. It said to me, 'I am already twenty and have been hard-working and not pleasure-seeking in the past. My future seems likely to be the same. But I am worth no less than others... Why should this be my fate.' However, I know, Lord, that the stone does not choose where it will be used, the Master of the work does this... I fit in well here, so here I will stay. I am happy and peaceful because I do not belong to myself."

The letters he received were not kept with his papers but it is easy to guess that this very gifted sister felt shut in, there in the village. Was she fated to grow old on this barren soil? Maurice encouraged her to be patient and invited her to shed light around her in this little kingdom by remaining peaceful, since even the most obscure existence has meaning and value before God.

The years spent at St Maurice show us how patiently Maurice Tornay worked on himself from the time he was fifteen till he was twenty-one. He did well in his studies and his teachers and supervisors were satisfied with his behaviour in spite of certain slips that they willingly pardoned. "We did not wish to punish him for his occasional outbursts for he was a very good student," they commented. He struggled against his fiery nature and his inclination to profit of the ability to lead his companions.

The mission of the college was not to level down personalities by imposing uniformity but, on the contrary, respecting differences to build on the originality of each. This was well done at St Maurice then for there was a team of remarkable young teachers who formed generations of students later to become famous in various fields.

Often Maurice was not punished even for his most serious outbursts. The supervisor was not blind to them, but he reasoned with him about them and suggested he should try to correct them. His frankness, sign of his deep moral honesty, and the fact that he was not resentful led him to distance himself from his first reaction, caused more by his quick temper than by his reason or heart. Then he would excuse himself to the companions who had followed his lead. That was more effective than a punishment which might be imposed exteriorly without being accepted interiorly.

During the final years of his secondary education Maurice progressed in self-knowledge and in smoothing certain aspects of his character which he recognised as being major obstacles to his vocation. He was then sure he wanted to become a priest and did not even wait till his final year to speak to the Abbot about it.

When a young man goes to a college like that run by the Canons of the Abbey of St Maurice and does not hide the fact that he is attracted by the religious vocation, he is generally given a priest to direct him. No mention is made of a director in Maurice's case, but this is probably because this person was also his confessor. However, Maurice did not hesitate to mention in his letters his joy in following the annual retreats and to share the benefits of them with those to whom he wrote.

When at college, Maurice joined the Organization of the Children of Mary and the Society of Swiss Students, an association which prepares young people for political life and Christian social action.

In May 1930, when he was twenty, he went on a pilgrimage to Lourdes and was greatly moved by this experience. The sufferings of those he saw at the grotto or the baths upset him but helped him to realise that this life is only the preparation for the next and to accept that ugliness and splendour can exist side by side. "Eternal life has never seemed so clear to me and the present has never seemed so beautiful. I cannot speak of it, nor weep human tears but my heart and soul express themselves simply by sorrow and prayer."

This was not a show of maudlin religiosity. Mountain folk generally tend to stifle too open a display of tenderness. However, Maurice showed by the feelings that moved him at Lourdes that under a tough shell he had a lively sensitivity. A witness noted, "He was very hard on himself wanting to conquer himself and he was extremely mortified." This was no isolated remark, yet under Maurice's tough exterior was a tender heart.

At the sight of suffering, human misery, appeals for help from the wounded and also on the missions when he saw the children of his mission station in rags, hungry and badly treated and knew that the Christians of Yerkalo were forced to apostasize, Maurice was moved to re-live the night of Gethsemane.

It is not by force of will one becomes a saint but by love. Because human love has been wounded, it will always meet with suffering. "Do not imagine you can love without suffering and without much suffering."[1]

29

Did Maurice Tornay already want to be a missionary when he left college? Some people think that he did. All that can be said is that he knew he had a rebellious nature to conquer and he had perhaps asked himself whether religious life in Europe would give him a chance to reach his highest possibilities. St Thérèse became a saint in Carmel by a sublime interior path. The only possibility for Maurice, as he would confide later to his brother, seemed to be to go away: "I must go far away and work with all my strength to do God's will, not wanting to be noticed or spoken of, so as to give myself completely through pure love of God."

We will come back to this later. The final step before his entry as novice in the Great St Bernard Abbey was his letter of 12 July 1931 to Mgr Bourgeois, the Abbot of the Congregation in which he asked to enter. Since he must have weighed every word and only written it after examining his situation and the call he had received, it seems indispensable to quote this important document in full.

Monsignor,

To answer my vocation which is to leave the world to give myself completely to the service of souls in order to lead them to God and to ensure my salvation, very humbly I come to ask you, Monsignor, to accept me as a novice in the Great St Bernard Abbey.

I am convinced that here is my place. But if you accept me I know it is not because of this conviction, nor thanks to my merits, for these are non-existent. It is thanks to the vocation that you yourself foster as do all in the Abbey, so that those who leave their parents, their brothers and their goods may be enabled to follow Jesus.

Thus I hope to be received and I promise you, Monsignor, that I truly desire to be stripped of myself and to become a priest of St Augustine and worthy to obey your orders.

Please believe in the sincerity of a young man who would like to become your spiritual son, Monsignor, and bless him as he kisses your ring.

Tornay Maurice

All is explained without unnecessary emphasis and in an orderly manner: the call to leave the world to devote himself to the service of souls and to realise his own salvation; the spirit of humility; the choice of this Abbey so near and yet so far from the world, which should help him to forget himself; the respect for St Augustine, who was both a mystic and an untiring apostle in North Africa, a Father of the Church and Father Founder of the order of the Augustines to whom the Canons of the Great St Bernard are attached: all this indeed shows clearly what his desire really was.

At this time there were plenty of vocations. The Congregation was renewed regularly as one novice each year sufficed to assure the future of the community. Maurice was received with three other postulants, one of whom was the future Abbot, Mgr Angelin Lovey. This unexpected growth may be due to the fact that the Foreign Mission Society of Paris (FMP) had just asked the Canons of the Great St Bernard Abbey to collaborate with them in a work they had undertaken in Tibet since 1846.

The climatic conditions and the problems caused by the altitude and the situation of the land had led the superiors of the FMP, to ask the Vatican for help that would answer the specific needs of this apostolate in a high mountain region. Pius XI who had been a great alpinist before his election as Pope, quite naturally thought of the famous Hospice of Mount Joux and suggested that Mgr de Guebriant, Superior of the FMP should write to the Great St Bernard Abbey. An agreement was reached fairly rapidly and this called for new forces in the Congregation.

In any case, Maurice Tornay was expected at the Abbey towards the end of August 1931, several days before his clothing ceremony arranged for 25 August.

Before we accompany him to the Hospice as he leaves the world, let us go up once again with him to Cretes and say farewell to his family. His sister Marie in her testimony remembers this as the most moving moment of their separation: "I wanted him to go to the Great St Bernard Abbey, but all the same I said to him: Stay with us, Maurice! I will be left alone with Josephine. I do not have the same ideas as John, whereas if we were together we could do much good. He answered that there was something far greater than all the beauties of the earth. He added that Christ had said that the Gospel must be preached to the very ends of the earth. Already, as he was about to enter the Great St Bernard Abbey, he felt the call of the missions, but he never spoke clearly to us about it."

In 1928, his sister Anna, two years his junior, had entered religious life, when she was only sixteen, in the Congregation of the Sisters of Charity of La Roche-sur-Foron. This event touched Maurice deeply. He realised both the joy but also the sorrow the family, particularly his mother, would feel when in offering a child to God she would leave home for good. His own plan to enter St Bernard Abbey was known and approved. In fact, as he began his secondary studies in 1925, he had already been presented to the Abbot of the Congregation by his parents. But if, as his sister Marie thought, the desire to become a missionary was growing and strengthening during the years he spent in college, it seems natural that he did not speak of it. He would not want to worry his mother uselessly as long as the plan was no more definite than a dream. He revealed it at the last minute to his sister when answering her cry of "stay with us".

This must have pierced him like an unexpected arrow coming from Marie, to whom he had written letters asking her to share his commitment and to help him to realise it.

The Twenties were decisive in the evolution of his missionary vocation. We will not say much here, except to recall that during the pontificate of Pius XI 1(922-1939) after his encyclical, *Rerum Ecclesiae* (28 February 1926) the urgent need to form and institute an indigenous clergy in all the mission lands had become really pressing.

In this same year, on 28 October 1926, the Pope welcomed six Chinese priests and consecrated them bishops. The Holy Father availed of this event to reveal the lack of foundation of the arguments of those "who tended to represent Catholic preaching as a foreign commodity, or as an instrument of domination in the service of the European Powers."[2] This was a turning point in missionary psychology. The vocation of Maurice Tornay ripened in this new context.

Away to become a saint

In the clothing ceremony the novice exchanges his lay clothes for the cassock and surplice. The prelate who presided spoke these words of the ritual as the symbolic gesture was made:

"May God strip you of the old man and his deeds. May God clothe you with the new man fashioned according to his plans, so that you may resemble Christ in justice and holiness."

Among the questions which the postulant answered, note the following:

"Do you realise how serious is the commitment you undertake in religious life?"

The firm voice of Maurice, heard clearly by his family, friends and future companions, gave this answer:

"I do realise this. I know that by myself I can do nothing but I trust completely in the grace of our Lord. He has said that His yoke is easy and his burden light for those who, giving up the world, follow him with all their heart."

The next day Maurice began his noviciate under the Novice Master, Fr Nestor Adam, future Abbot (1939-1952), and later Bishop of Sion (952-1977). On 11 October 1931, just a month and a half later, Maurice wrote to his family: "Before I entered I said to myself, 'You will be like a prisoner behind walls on the top of a mountain' and yet I have never felt so free. I do exactly what I want, since God's will is shown me at each moment and I want only to do this will. I think how good God is to leave me so close to you. I asked myself whether I belonged sufficiently to Him. He answered that it was his affair if he chose to give me so many good things. All the better, I will become holy almost in your midst if I try hard and if you pray for me."

The noviciate is a critical period in the life of a religious. One learns detachment, renunciation and obedience. The Novice Master has to test candidates for their aptitude. We know what the time-table was in the Great St Bernard Hospice at that time. The rising bell went at 5 am in summer and 5.30 in winter. Before breakfast there was half an hour's meditation kneeling on the bare boards, then the Little Hours were recited, followed by the Conventual Mass. During the morning the novice made a half hour's spiritual reading and had to render account of this the following Sunday. Then came study and an instruction from the Novice Master between nine and eleven. Next was preparation and singing of the Office according to the Solesmes method. After a short break the novices went to the Church for examination of conscience and Midday Office. During the meals they were responsible for the reading and the service. In the afternoon there was a visit to the Blessed Sacrament, recitation of the rosary, then study until four. Later came a long celebration during which Vespers, and Compline were sung and Matins and Lauds were recited. The evening was given over to the Way of the Cross, spiritual reading and general culture. Once a week there was an excursion from nine until six.

Here was a school for character-building based on oblation, sacrifice, prayer and study. "When Maurice Tornay wrote to his family, 'I do what I want...', he showed that these exacting demands corresponded with what he sought and that he was sufficiently committed psychologically to his vocation to succeed in making the transition from the full freedom of Cretes to the monastery cloister. From the beginning he was not content simply to satisfy all the constraints which he felt were light, but wanted to rush ahead along the path of perfection. His Novice Master has never forgotten the question Maurice asked him insistantly, "What must I do to become holy?"

It would be interesting to know what answer his Novice Master, gave him, especially since he had been warned that this young man had a very difficult character. The Novice

Master's testimony about him leaves no ambiguity: "I was very pleased with him during the whole of his noviciate. He seemed to me to be animated by a sincere desire to work at his perfection."

Let us now glance rapidly over the final stages of Maurice Tornay's religious and priestly formation, noting briefly what his programme was from the time he entered the Great St Bernard Abbey.

— 25 August 1931: he began his noviciate and took the habit of the Congregation of the Canons of St Augustine.

— 8 September 1932: he made his simple profession and began his study of philosophy which lasted two years.

— October 1934: he started his theological studies which lasted for four years.

— 8 September 1935: he made his solemn profession.

— 15 September 1935: he received the tonsure and the minor orders.

— February 1938: he finished his theological studies in Yunnan.

— 20 April 1938: he was made subdeacon and two days later, was ordained deacon.

— 24 April 1938: he was ordained priest in Hanoi by Mgr Chaize.

— 3 July 1938: he celebrated his first Mass in Siao-Weisi.

We will complete this chronological list by two events which can be noted without upsetting the order: from January to August 1935, he was in the Bois-Cerf Hospital in Lausanne and had an operation in the Cecil Clinic at the end of January followed by several months of convalescence at Martigny. On 24 February 1936, he sailed from Marseille for China and arrived at Weisi on 8 May 1936 where he continued his theological studies. Between May 1936 and July 1938 he also learnt Chinese.

Many testimonies were given about this part of his life, just as there had been during his years in college. Robert

Loup noted what Mgr Adam himself said, soon after the death of the Servant of God. "He was very original but with nothing displeasing about this. … His lively mind, his unexpected answers and the validity of his intuitions were evident. Maurice Tornay had a combative temperament characterised by both a kind of quick impetuosity and a rugged frankness. But I must state that of all the novices, he was the one who was the most transformed, the most disciplined and the one who aimed the most seriously at perfection. In spite of his independent nature, his obedience was truly admirable. I do not say this simply because of his heroic death which crowned his exemplary life."

What a portrait! Mgr Adam was known always to weigh his words, and how strongly he spoke here. It seemed as if the prelate, looking back over this life in the light of its tragic end, spoke straight from his heart. It is the same Maurice we have seen in childhood and in college, with his contradictions, his outbursts, already harmonised and integrated in the wonderful plan of this life and seeming to be almost indispensable for its fulfilment.

The Chief Recorder for the Cause of the Servant of God, Fr Ambroise Eszer OP notes appositely that if Maurice Tornay had an impetuous and choleric temperament which he tried to dominate, "it was precisely this temperament which helped him and gave him the strength to live as the only European missionary in a vast country faced with the almost general animosity of the religious and civil authorities; to learn two extremely difficult languages, Chinese and Tibetan, quite different from each other; and to show extraordinary perseverance in enduring this solitude. When Fr Tornay was Yerkalo's parish priest living within the boundaries of forbidden Tibet, these qualities were apparent.

Canon Lucien Gabioud who became Prior of the Hospice, was his philosophy professor from 1932 to 1934. He emphasised his gift for studies, the clarity of his mind and his need to get to the bottom of things. The paradoxical side of his nature, his mischievousness, was always

37

present in spite of the gravity of his commitment and the rigour of life in the monastery. "He was very good at asking awkward questions even of his professors and he delighted to do so... Both his superiors and his companions thought highly of him."

He continued to share with his family both his cares and his joys. But he asked them to be detached from material goods so as to free their hearts which should belong entirely to God. "What you have ploughed you will have to leave one day: all you love will fall into someone else's hands. Of course you should love the earth, but only in so far as it may lead us to God."

He meditated on the inevitable end of every life with his sister Anna, religious in France: "We are young, we are twenty years old, we love God, we have nothing to fear from death: be happy! ... We must make haste, mustn't we? At our age others have already become saints. If the stem bears flowers for too long the fruit cannot ripen before the cold and death approach: and there are so many sinners, so many pagans who call to us and whom we want to answer. Our very flesh and blood belongs to them. I tell you again: We must make haste. The longer I live the more I am convinced that sacrifice alone gives meaning to our days."

The first Christmas away from his family Maurice wrote a long letter to the whole household. A remark made by his mother before he left came back to his mind: "When you are far away from us we will no longer be happy at Christmas time." He comments: "It takes a mother to speak like that. I rejoiced to think of your loving kindness. But what you say is not really Christian. I would not like to take or to hold the place of God in your hearts. I give it to him as he is the only one to whom it rightfully belongs. You offered me to him; each one offered me, so each one has merited eternal life and the hundredfold in this world... Remember that all pleasures are deceptive, absolutely all of them. Heaven alone can give us true happiness, not only free of all feeling of sadness but, above all, with everything we could hope for.

The more he advanced, the more insistent became the desire to give himself entirely to the call, to renounce himself, to become wholly committed to all that God wanted to accomplish through him. In the beginning there was perhaps the need to ensure his own salvation and that of those he loved. This seemed a desirable form of happiness. He had chosen a life which was difficult and demanding. To become a priest means to become a saint. His request to his family, "help me to be a holy priest", was often repeated.

He knew that the path of perfection follows the way of sacrifice. He wanted to rid himself of his ego so as to make a complete offering of himself to the Lord. He knew his weaknesses. Would he ever overcome them in following the common path? "I know that by myself I can do nothing...", he had said on his Clothing day. So he asked help from everyone. What could his parents, brothers and sisters and friends do, they who were so occupied with their own tasks and plans that they could not distance themselves from the pressures of daily life to think about the meaning of their actions and of their life? The answer to this question is found in most of the letters he wrote from the Great St Bernard Abbey with variations on the one theme summed up admirably in this invitation to his mother: "O Mama, offer some of your sufferings for me. That is the best of prayers..."

He reminded his sister Josephine that: "Our slightest sufferings have an infinite value if we unite them with those of Christ." He added this enlightening remark as a warning: "You know that I was never over credulous in religious matters. I have not changed, yet I can assure you what I am saying is true."

To his brother Louis who loved to help the missions he wrote: "That is good, but remember this: Only prayer can bring about conversion." He had just reminded his mother that sacrifice is prayer, now he continued to Louis: " When you deprive yourself of some dish or a glass of wine ... for the pagans, you do more than if you were to give a hundred francs each time. You merit to hear these words of Christ: 'I was thirsty and you gave me to drink'."

On 1 January 1933, he wrote to each member of his family and then he said to them all: "Offer your tears to God ... for the Missions ... And I beg of you all to help me by your prayers and sufferings to become a saint." He added humbly that he knew very well what was needed to become a saint but that he often lacked the courage to carry it out.

After having told his aged father that the land, "sees us pass without emotion" and so "there's nothing to get upset about", he suggested this simple spiritual exercise, which is nevertheless extremely demanding since the heart has to be changed: "... Each day, give some little sign of affection to the person you like the least, so that Christ's Kingdom may become more glorious. I will do this with you."

Fr Tornay's letters sketch the outline of a path, through offering and sacrifice, to achieve forgetfulness of self in love of others and the sanctification of joys and sorrows. It is a question of reaching holiness by advancing together bound by a common wish of self-giving. Thanks to the gift of self to each other, which is the communion of the saints on the move, those trying to become holy, who meet as they travel along their obscure path daily, can be certain that they share in the communion of the Mystical Body of Christ. They and those who are already in heaven are one because salvation is already accomplished.

In the quotations already given, the thought of the missions seems ever present. It is possible to affirm with almost complete certainty that Maurice Tornay was already thinking of leaving for the missions one day, whilst he was in his last years of college. As in every life, convergences and coincidences to which we must be attentive are apparent.

Towards the end of 1929 when Maurice was still in college, the Abbot of the Great St Bernard Abbey, Mgr Bourgeois, received the following letter from Mgr de Guebriant, Superior of the Foreign Missions of Paris:

Very Reverend Father,

When I paid a visit, last October, to the Abbey of St Maurice I was able to share with Mgr Marietan, an idea that I have had for the last thirty years. ... I spent thirty-one years in the furthermost province in the heart of China, at Setchouan on the Tibetan border, and during seventeen years I was responsible for a mountainous district called Kientchang. ... This area, twice as big as Switzerland, is no less mountainous. ... That will tell you that I am as familiar with mountain regions as are the religious of St Bernard. ...

How often, as I followed the caravans that went along these difficult tracks, I said to myself as I traversed dangerous passes, swept by snow and wind: "What a wonderful thing it would be to have here a hospice like that of the St Bernard Abbey, how useful and how beneficial it would be for the whole region.

I would assume that, obviously, you would need to send two of your religious to study the situation in the region I have mentioned, a journey which would take at least a whole year. ...

I would add that I am convinced such a journey, undertaken in the countries like those I mention, might suggest another way, in line with the traditions of your venerable Congregation, to exercise a fruitful and glorious apostolate for the Church.

Mgr Bourgeois wished to examine this possibility. He visited his correspondent, and afterwards sent two of the Canons in November 1930 to view the region of Yunnan. They were back at the Great St Bernard Abbey on 28 July 1931. A year and a half was needed to form the future missionaries and, on 13 January 1933, Canons Pierre-Marie Melly and Paul Coquoz, the two pioneers, together with Brother Louis Duc and Robert Maurice Chappelet, a layman who came from St Maurice, sailed from Marseille for Weisi in the Yunnan where they arrived on 1 April of the same year.

A glance at the letters of Maurice Tornay at that period shows that they revolve round two great projects: *to become holy and to become a missionary*. These two dreams combined in his mind, little by little, to form one and the same project which was henceforth to be the great adventure of his life. But it still remained a secret. Certainly he never hid his desire to reach perfection. It is also true that he spoke more and more frequently of the missions in his letters. He even mentioned his wish to some of his companions, to a few former students who came to see him and also to his brother Louis. But he saw clearly that too many obstacles stood in the way of a swift realisation of his dream.

The two main obstacles were his poor health and the time that still had to elapse before his ordination. For a long time he had been in great pain following a stomach ulcer which, even at St Maurice, had already troubled him. In 1934, it became much worse. Without interruption the studies would last until 1938, only then would he become a priest and perhaps have a chance to realise his plans.

However, his persistence must not be forgotten. During 1934-1935, he felt convinced that his destiny depended on the realisation of this wish to go to the missions as soon as possible. Why this urgency? It seems that no-one had actually asked him this until the eve of his departure in 1936. That evening Canon Lucien Gabioud, his former philosophy professor, met him by chance at Martigny and got him to express his innermost thoughts. Here is the secret we will speak of later. Maurice had discovered that he could not become holy unless he gave up everything by becoming a missionary at the other end of the world and in the most difficult conditions that could be imagined.

When it was decided that he should go, he confided to his brother Louis: "To develop into someone, I must go away. Here I can come to see you... I will be spoiled by this one or the other, and this will not help me. I must go away, because it will be so much easier to work at my sanctification away from the family." During this same conversation which took place near the bridge over the Rhone at St Maurice (for Louis was then living with his family at Lavey) he made the matter clearer: "I would like to wear myself out, through pure love for God. My dear Louis, I will never come back once I have gone away."

But let us not anticipate. During the last months of 1934, his health became so bad that he had to be hospital-ised. On 11 January 1935, he wrote to his Prior from the Bois-Cerf Clinic in Lausanne that the doctor had diagnosed "a small duodenal ulcer". He would need either an opera-tion or three weeks treatment. On 25 January, Doctor Roux told him an operation was necessary and would take place three days later in the Cecil Clinic.

He reassured his parents: "Pray that this operation may be useful for my salvation. ... In any case, if I die I will go to heaven; if I do not die I will see you in about a month."

He did not mention his ulcer when writing to his brother on the same day, but spoke about holiness: "If you could only realise how many difficulties, sorrows and dangers a soul meets when working at perfection! Truly heroic strength is needed, even in the smallest matters. ... Let us never forget we are on a journey and that the only way to become holy is through detachment and death."

The next day he wrote to his Prior: "I feel my flesh is indeed weak. It is not without danger that a young religious leaves his monastery. Vain and useless conversations are easier than meditation; to talk about oneself, more flatter-ing than to be recollected. How I long to rejoin my dear Hospice and what a lot of pruning I still need to do."

Still he went on planning. Even before the operation he hoped his superiors would realise that this was only a passing affair which did not undermine any of his plans for the future. First the operation, then ten days' convales-cence in the Cecil Clinic, three weeks at Bois-Cerf and six months on a diet, and "the machine will be ready to work as new. I can picture it speeding over mountains and through valleys. It is only the mountains and plains of Tibet that will be able to stop it."

His stay in Lausanne lasted longer than expected since Maurice only left the clinic on 10 March. He was not able to go straight back to his community, but first spent four months of rest in Martigny. He was anxious about his interrupted theological studies and wanted to prepare for the yearly examinations in July. He wrote to his Prior: "Please give my best wishes to the theology students and tell them I hope they will shine brighter than ever in their examinations, and they may be sure that I will be the most stupid of them all."

These playful remarks reveal, all the same, how uneasy he was at the interruption to his studies, because the doctor had limited the time he spent in "hard" work to between two and a half to three hours per day. He also had to rest a great deal and follow a strict diet.

His long stay in the clinic gave Maurice the chance to write to each of his brothers and sisters. He was more pressing than ever in urging them not to lose sight of life's aim. He felt he was the object of much loving solicitude. "It is quite amusing to be ill! ... It is also the path to eternity..." He was not just making pious remarks but speaking of a reality he already lived in anticipation. Later on in a letter written to Marie, he imagines himself in heaven. "I think that one day I will present you to St Joseph. I will say to him: 'Here is my sister, Mary. It is she who prepared my room when I went home; she who worked hard to buy books for me so that I might become a priest; she who wept the most bitterly when I left for the monastery and who used to cry when she read my letters. Now, good guardian of heaven, let this humble Christian enter so that she may at last enjoy infinite happiness with you for ever."

In this letter he put a note in for each one. His total gift of himself belonged to them. Without them he would never have been able to offer it. All that they had lived together would be part of their happiness when they were finally reunited in heaven. "I will be in heaven with you, dear John. We will go together to God our Father's heavenly home. ... And then, John, just as at Cretes when the sun went down and the animals were at peace, and peace too reigned between us, so we will look at each other with everlasting and quite inconceivable joy."

He did not speak in this way because of the gravity of the moment because he viewed the prospect of his operation and possible death with great serenity. All the letters he wrote from Bois-Cerf were uplifting. His mind seemed elevated, freed from anxiety, and filled with an almost euphoric breath of the Spirit. He did not consider that the cotton-wool atmosphere of the clinic or the magic of medicines had played much part in his recovery. He suggested for a sister who was sick: "She should spend a few days at Cretes as it is difficult to get better in a convalescent home. Sickness creates a setting very difficult to overcome."

When he was stopped in mid-course, he found his uncertainty about the urgency of his call to the missions was difficult to accept. His greatest desire was to have Mgr Bourgeois' authorisation to leave as soon as possible, even before his ordination which was planned for 1938. He knew letters were being received from Tibet asking for reinforcements and he had also heard that the Abbot had replied that he had no-one to send at that moment.

In August 1935, as soon as he was back in the Hospice he began to prepare for his solemn profession fixed for 8 September. At that time nothing had yet been decided about the future and he wrote to his parents to ask them to come for his final vows. He was afraid that it might be too tiring for his mother to climb up to the Hospice and he wanted to reassure her: "Besides, it will not be my last feast. It seems probable that I will not leave for the mission before I am ordained."

He submits but does not give up. To one of his former college companions at St Maurice whose family was related to Mgr Bourgeois he wrote: "When Mgr Bourgeois visits you, do what you can in my favour so that I will be able to leave for the Mission."

We must believe that the Holy Spirit enlightened the Abbot since he had many reasons not to favour Maurice's early departure. In fact, having given in to M. Melly's insistence, he had conditionally suggested what he himself recognised as a halting solution: "I have a priest, Canon Lattion, a theology student, M. Maurice Tornay, and a Brother, M. Nestor Rouiller. M. Tornay's health is not good and his doctor advises against his departure."

But M. Melly was asking for help and not additional work and he answered to this proposition that a seminarian would take up a priest's valuable time as his studies would need supervision. This could not be thought of in a difficult mission situation.

Time passed. On September, Maurice committed himself solemnly by pronouncing the three vows of poverty, chastity and obedience. The promise of the young professed monk, spoken in presence of the large crowd that had come to the Hospice on this great occasion, concluded thus: "O God, may you receive the sacrifice I make of myself as a pleasing holocaust, and as you have secretly inspired me to make this offering, give me sufficient grace to accomplish it..."

All obstacles seemed to disappear very rapidly. What had happened? Undoubtedly the machine that even before his operation Maurice had imagined going full speed, seemed to answer his optimistic forecast fully. When he heard missionaries would soon be leaving, he must have done all he could to be one of them. Whatever happened, suddenly all Mgr Bourgeois' hesitations disappeared leaving him fully convinced that the group of pioneers in Yunnan had to be helped. An opportunity occurred and Maurice took it gladly: "Tornay insists: his health has improved, the doctor thinks he could undertake the voyage and that the climate of Asia would suit him. As for his formation, do not be anxious. He is a chosen subject and could work on his own. You can count completely on his tenacity. The three missionaries will leave Martigny in February 1936."

Everything seemed to work out according to his cherished wish, so Maurice knew he had been heard. Life is not made up of scattered fragments that we try to stick together. We see in all the decisive moments of Maurice's life that without any concessions his free will chose to work to reach the end he had perceived so early. There is an impenetrable mystery here, that grace, a gift from heaven, together with the light of the Spirit will be present in this great plan and yet his personal freedom will have full play.

Maurice was soon to leave. From the photos of this period we see his gaze fixed already far beyond the present. During the next four or five months he had some training with a doctor and a dentist to prepare for departure as the missionary had to be capable of alleviating human misery first of all. He was thrilled by this formation even though it was so rapid and once he was on the mission he would become for everyone the one who healed and restored life.

He still had to accomplish his most difficult task, that of taking leave of his family. He also wanted to see his sister Anna, a religious in France, and to receive her final encouragement by way of a send-off that would make him feel free when the rest of his family tried to hold him back. The sister's testimony shows clearly what a dilemma she had to face: "I asked him why he had to leave so soon, just at that moment... He said to me: 'Is that the answer you give me, I who hoped to receive encouragement from you?' I told him I was happy that he was chosen, but that the thought of my parents had prompted my remark. He answered: 'It is absolutely necessary. Nothing is ever too much to do for God.'"

Then came his last night at La Rosiere and a sleepless one. His mother had the strength not to weep. Farewells continued along the road to Orsieres where he was accompanied by his two sisters, Marie and Josephine. Marie recalled their final words: "I told him to take all he could from home, a little mountain air and the stars we could see here. He said that he had everything. I asked him what he would do when no-one was there to help him... He answered by singing the Magnificat and we burst into tears..."

Freedom must also pass through suffering. Grace supports the one but does not take away the other. Maurice was to write: "I felt the exquisite point of all sufferings."

Map of the region where Blessed Maurice Tornay worked

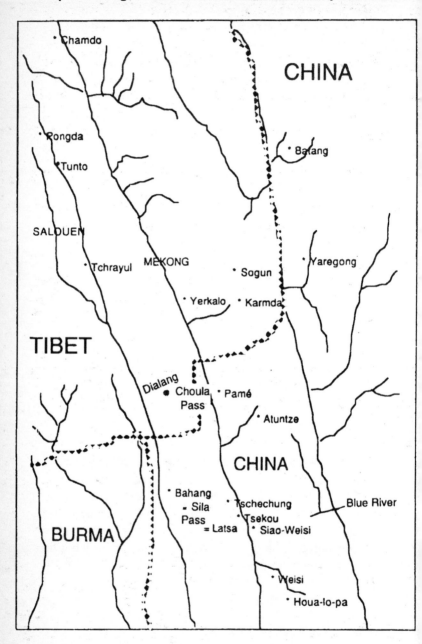

Departure for Yunnan

On 4 February 1936, Maurice Tornay, with Fr Lattion and Br Nestor Rouiller, left Marseille on board a ship for China. This "house bigger than the church in Orsieres", carried towards its fulfilment a far-seeing man who had been a missionary in his heart from his seminary days. It was not just a dream of adventure that was being realised for him, but the fulfilment of his dearest wish: to become holy in a distant land far away from the attractions of a comfortable middle-class life, such as he might have met in a Valais parish.

He set out. He followed the same path as his predecessors, Fathers Melly and Coquoz, Br Duc and M. Chappelet. His destination was Weisi in the Chinese province of Yunnan. The word 'mission', dear to his family and his parish but which still had a naïve and somewhat abstract meaning for himself, little by little became real. The veil was torn aside. He was the one this time, sent to spread "the true faith in the world", as Pius XI had desired. He was also the "worker-missionary" who was to make the future hospice a place that would have real influence by carrying out the tasks similar to those in the Great St Bernard Hospice. There would be hospitality for travelling merchants, in a place where they would be safe from danger and at the same time where the constant praise of God would resound. Mgr de Guebriant had longed for this ever since 1918, when he had seen in Setchuoan, just how difficult it was for the caravans to cross the dangerous passes safely. Maurice the missionary knew he would depend on the Foreign Missions of Paris and that he would be collaborating with a masterful and prudent man, Fr Francis Gore who lived in Tsechung.

The young student in theology had left behind the security of the Hospice walls and his fraternal community. If La Rosiere was where he was rooted, Cretes the origin of his vocation and his family the place where everything was given him, today resolutely he broke with his past without excluding it out from his heart but rather using it as a blessed step to reach the final goal: a priest serving God and his neighbour totally.

The voyage was long: two and a half months. The boat went from port to port: Port Said, Djibouti, Colombo in the Indian Ocean, Singapore, Saigon, the Gulf of Tonkin and Haiphong. It is easy to imagine young Maurice's bewilderment, he who had only left Switzerland once before to go on pilgrimage to Lourdes in 1930. However, this voyage was the necessary passage from Mont-Joux to the far distant Weisi to which he felt called and where the Fathers, overwhelmed by work, were waiting for their arrival.

As the days of the journey seemed to stretch out unendingly, more propitious to prayer, leisure or writing than anything else, the future missionary made use of it to strengthen his resolve. He had left his father, mother, brothers and sisters, his friends and above all his beloved community of the Great St Bernard behind him, but he did not look back filled with vain regrets. Already his heart had crossed the oceans. He wrote to tell them that everything was going well and that they should not waste time in useless anxiety. His vocation lay in the land of the mission, it was there he would work for the outcast, there that he would achieve his own salvation and that of all those entrusted to him. The young seminarian gazed into the unknown future, saw his road to holiness and ignored the conviction he had often felt and had even mentioned to his brother Louis, that he would never return from Tibet.

Such was Maurice Tornay as people knew him in La Rosiere, at Cretes, at St Maurice, then in the seminary. The voyage only served to reinforce the traits of his character: his generosity, will-power, energy, occasional impetuosity, his strength, courage and his perseverance in seeking to improve. He loved the land he had left behind, but he loved much more the One who had led him to the dizzy heights of sacrifice. Holding on to the handrail, he looked beyond the horizon, and turned his back on mediocrity. Was his name not Maurice like the leader of the Thebian legion, who was martyred because he would not apostasize? He had no fears about what lay ahead, rather he was impatient to reach the goal: already God filled the whole place.

On 25 March, the missionary team reached Hanoi. Before them lay an unknown, almost hostile land with no security or guarantees, a land enduring the plague of continual war. Yunnan belonged to China and the communist devastation had begun there more than ten years earlier. Sometimes the communists fled from the Nationalist Army of Tchiang Kai Chek, sometimes they even joined forces with them to thrust back the menace of the Japanese expansion. That very year, 1936, Yunnanfou fell into the hands of the communists and there were rumours that they were going to remount the Blue River. Thus even before he landed, Maurice was drawn into the whirlwind of war.

Normally, it took about twenty-five days to reach Weisi from Hanoi, but in time of war it could take much longer. The new arrivals were plunged immediately into the climate of uncertainty which would later weigh on them and their entry in Weisi, on 8 May, was most unusual. They were already three weeks late, worn out from the journey along places "as steep as the track the cripples made to climb up to Cretes". In addition they found no-one at the mission to welcome them. They had to begin by breaking down the doors, for the Fathers awaiting them had been obliged to flee towards Loutzekiang or Salouen, taking with them whatever valuables they wanted to save from the expected pillage. The entire population had deserted the Mekong valley. Fathers Melly and Coquoz were able to stop at Tsechung, with Fr Gore. Thus the meeting at Weisi did not take place! Maurice Tornay remained hopeful and confident, judging that there was nothing surprising in such a situation in time of war. Ten days later, after many detours along some 400 kilometres, the elders saw the new team approaching them along a valley that they had unexpectedly discovered. Imagine the joy of those first moments of a meeting that had seemed impossible! The communist thrust had spread to the north towards Batang without touching Mekong so for the moment the mission was no longer in danger.

This perilous arrival made Maurice think about death. In fact, since he went on board at Marseille, it seems likely the thought had never left him nor that of the journey towards the absolute which was his reason for living. But the absolute can only be reached through the ultimate sacrifice. For him, eternal life always seemed more important than this temporal life. He had already written to his brother Louis in 1927 "...The day of our death is the happiest of our life. We must be glad about it above all things since it means we will arrive in our true fatherland." Was this foreknowledge? Not necessarily, for a missionary encounters danger daily. God becomes the sovereign good for which the servant is ready to give everything, even his life.

Weisi: study and action

To situate Weisi, subject to both Chinese and Tibetan influences, we must follow the Red River as far as Lac Tali. To the east lies the main town of Yunnanfou. Then the valley of the Yang-tse-Kiang or the Blue River opens out before us. Were we to traverse the Litipin Pass we would finally see the great valley running parallel with that of Mekong. This was the path taken by the new missionary team. The little town of Weisi lay not far from a small valley at about 2350 metres. It was in the north-west of Yunnan Province and had about two thousand five hundred inhabitants of whom about eighty were Christians.

The mountains and the great rivers, sprung from an ancient sea set at the very heart of Tibet, lie close by. The Mekong flows almost parallel to the Blue River, to the Salouen and to the Irawaddi which will take different directions downstream. In spite of the great flow of water the valleys are narrow and steep, and their torrents swollen by the thawing of the ice and snow can be most impressive. The hydrographic system as it was before the great upheaval of the mountains of "the Roof of the World" has not changed and this explains why the watershed does not coincide with the line of mountain summits. The torrents, streams and rivers overcame by their swiftness the uplifting of the land and defended their courses, drop by drop. That is why there are gigantic gorges cutting into the land which was raised from out of the bowels of the Tibetan land. Thus between the rivers lie the high mountains and there are passes at a height of more than 5000 metres. Here, the layout of the land determines all methods of travel, and shapes the merchants' journeys, their commercial activities and their meetings. It would be foolish to under-estimate the land. Following the Mekong river the servant of God and his missionary team passed through Tsechung, Merechu and Pame, finally reaching Yerkalo on the other side of the Sino-Tibetan border, which was the only Christian settlement in the territory called, "Land of the Spirits".

If we speak of Tibet we immediately think of the Himalayas, a place of great upheavals and chaos, resulting from the collision between Indian and Chinese plates about forty-five million years ago. Let us now leave the mighty summits which reach 11,000 metres and let us return to the Tibetan borderland. This region, rich in salt, was coveted by both China and Tibet, but in 1912, when there was a revolution against the foreign dynasty, the Tibetans, helped by the British from India, expelled the Chinese from the region. Tibet remained an independent state until 1951 when the Red Army over-ran Lhasa.

This is the country that the missionaries from Valais saw spread out before them. A new country to them, but which showed some similarities with Valais. The austere land, the rocky countryside, the cereals cultivated in the fields on the heights and the simple nature of the inhabitants, their way of life, their ingenuity in taking advantage of the least thing to help them survive, all this meant that our missionaries did not feel too much out of their element.

If we only studied the land from a geographical point of view, we certainly would not understand it. Why would young members from the Foreign Missions of Paris and from the Great St Bernard Abbey volunteer to come to Yunnan and try to advance into Tibetan territory if not to plant the Cross? Just as St Bernard of Menthon sought when founding the Hospice bearing his name in the 11th century, so the missionaries likewise sought that the planting of the Cross of Christ would bring liberation and hope to a people who had been ruled over by a power which, instead of serving, had exploited them and reduced them to conditions of life similar to that in Europe during the Middle Ages.

This was a bold venture to be undertaken by the

missionaries when the whole region was under the sway of a totalitarian Buddhism which was unwilling to allow the people to hear of any other religion, particularly with proselytising Catholicism. The ideas of the Church at that period were clearly reflected here. Unfortunately, in the past, the Church had the tendency to measure its success and spiritual growth by the number of baptisms and conversions obtained. When the Church sent out missionaries it took Christ's command, "Go and teach all nations," quite literally. Religious institutes often used as their charter for the spreading of the Gospel Benedict XV's Encyclical *Maximum Illud*, promulgated in 1919.

Most of the attempts at evangelisation in this region of the Middle Empire, especially from the 14th century, did not last. During an earlier period the missionaries were expelled relentlessly or even killed by the Lamas. In the middle of the 19th century, the Foreign Missions of Paris, already established in the Chinese Province of Sinkiang to the east of Tibet, were told to move into the forbidden territory. Ten priests were killed during this brave attempt, the missions were pillaged and set on fire and the Christians molested. Yerkalo remained the only mission on Tibetan soil and this too was persecuted by the Lamas. In the theocracy they had restored, the Lamas had both temporal and spiritual authority and possessed vast tracts of land; moreover they imposed a feudal sytem which reduced the people to serfdom and sometimes to complete slavery.

The Lamas, a term which means, "none are superior to us", were maintained by the faithful. In addition to them and to their supreme leader, the Dalai-Lama, both a political government and an army existed. Laws were promulgated, but the administration was systematically manipulated by the person who was the re-incarnation of Buddha. Another quasi-divinity, called the Panchen-Lama was charged to preserve doctrinal purity of the teachings of the Buddha. In the course of their history there were sometimes violent clashes between the two authorities.

The Lamas of Yunnan and the south east of Tibet,

whom the missionaries would have to face, were men perverted by many influences such as witchcraft, fetishism, magic, simony and superstition. Sometimes the Fathers had to try to find the difference between what the Lamas taught and pure paganism or even satanism. To understand their difficulties and dilemma it is important to take stock of the atmosphere of the years 1930-1950. It was not easy at that time to see values in non-Christian religions and not to condemn anything that had not its origin in Christ.

Some of the leaders did not hesitate to kill those who annoyed them and thus they showed they were far from practising true primitive Buddhism. Buddha in fact taught total respect for all forms of life, for goodness, kindness, piety, a whole new wisdom which should lead to interior perfection and, through transmigration, to reincarnation and *nirvána*.

This early Buddhism attached great importance to prayer and promised those who practised it a whole invisible world. At the same time their faith was supported by statues, buildings, carved stones and other visible signs. Does this not resemble Catholicism to a certain extent? Some of the priests showed their foresight by seeking points of convergence between the Buddhist and Christian ethic, instead of condemning everything.

The Lamas the missionaries encountered, lived in villages in really magnificent mansions, perched high on the cliffs like nests of eagles. Their lamaseries were carefully constructed and were flourishing centres of religious life where one could meet soldiers become monks, farmers become monks and monks who were mystics. They celebrated many feasts and during processions they took their holy books from the libraries and carried them in procession to the feet of some Buddha statue or other.

However, many of the Lamas came to the lamasery to escape the daily struggles of existence. They were showered with presents since they supposedly interceded for their followers with the various gods and spirits, appeased the heavenly powers and called down success and well-being on the faithful. They gradually became corrupt, greedy for possessions and power, and were, fanatical and quarrelsome. They should have sought perfection and waited for "Nirvana", that happiness that their renunciations should bring them. They terrorised the population and were often violent in seeking to achieve their aims to become lords of all and to recover their territorial fiefs.

These were the potentates whom the missionaries would confront when upholding the rights of the Christians entrusted to them and seeing that their most basic claims were met. They knew the Lamas would attempt the impossible to win back a Christian community once they had chased the parish priest away. They would force the little community to apostasize and would take the young boys from their families to make them bonzes or apprentices. They acted thus out of ignorance and hatred for the Catholic faith which, unlike Buddhism, they considered as a European religion. They were also jealous of their social privileges and used underhand tactics to avoid losing their influence over the people.

The poor people trembled as they served, maintained and obeyed them and burnt incense to obtain favour from and appease the gods. They disposed of the bodies of those who died or were killed as soon as possible so that their souls could be reincarnated. Thus they would throw the corpses into rivers, burn them or leave them on neighbouring mountains for the vultures to devour. Poor people, "seated in the shadow of death", it was towards them the missionaries came, with goodness and respect, to try to heal them and in so doing hoped to touch them spiritually as well. Their diocese then had no boundaries but was as wide as the dimensions of the universal Church.

Fr Tornay only needed a few weeks to size up the local situation completely. It was a desperate one both in Weisi and Yerkalo with, however, several little breathing spaces both in time and space to prove the truth of the words "The yoke of the Lord is easy and his burden light".

The Servant of God settled in the Chinese sub-prefecture of Weisi, on the left bank of the River of Eternal Spring, a tributary of the Mekong. He worked hard each day and tried to understand the mentality of the inhabitants, and how they managed to live under their very difficult conditions. He also continued his theological studies, guided by Fr Lattion. His superiors in the Great St Bernard Abbey had made him responsible for their completion. However, he saw that unless he learnt Chinese, he could neither be truly integrated, nor efficacious in medical care, in teaching the children, or in listening to and helping souls. At the end of a year he had learnt seven thousand characters for he was both determined and organised. He found his strength in adoration, meditation, prayer and the daily Mass which preceded his many hours of study.

He lived in the Mission Residence with Frs Melly and Lattion and with Br Rouiller. Since his operation for a stomach ulcer the previous year, his health had remained weak and he needed special attention even in the frugal meals imposed on them all by the season or by circumstances. Fr Melly had to ask him to follow the rules of the House without mitigations and it seemed as if his health improved under these difficulties and privations. He was so enthusiastic about his studies that his tutor had to hold him back. The young seminarian had to find his equilibrium to prepare for the task that awaited him.

On 25 June 1936, about a month after his arrival in China, he sat for his first theology examination and sustained the subjects of his oral test with resiliance. Fr Lattion could not but praise his constant and energetic efforts to carry out so many different activites whilst remaining faithful to his personal discipline. During the summer he studied hard to make up for the delay caused by the long voyage.

How did Fr Tornay get on as he worked among the people in this large village called Weisi. He tried to follow as closely as possible, the way the villagers lived which neither he nor his companions from Valais found too difficult since they all came from either country or mountain families. He knew how to care for animals, milk cows, make cheese, turn the soil, add fertilizers, sow, plant and harvest the grain, bake bread, use herbs to heal certain illnesses etc. He no longer wore the black cassock and white surplice as at the Abbey, but a simple robe without belt and he smoked a pipe in Chinese fashion. The villagers welcomed him warmly, liked to chat with him and became very attached to him. In church, he gave carefully prepared sermons in simple Chinese and the people listened with great attention. But what was hidden behind those flat and wrinkled brows?

The Father saw clearly that not all were sympathetic towards the Christian message and that most of the inhabitants came to the residence only when they needed money or medicine. They had no great need either for God or Buddha. They seemed concerned merely with this earthly life and he dreamt of gaining them for heaven. How could he make these indoctrinated souls feel thirst for spiritual truths? He had to begin by curing their physical illnesses, taking care of their ailments, and healing their wounds. Perhaps the rest would be given in addition, perhaps his good will would make up for his lack of preparation in every field. For he had to concede that the Great St Bernard Abbey did not have a real missionary tradition behind it as did the Institute from Paris, nor any experience of China.

When the Fathers left Valais, they could not speak the language and understood little of Oriental philosophy and spirituality. The term Lama meant nothing to them then. There were no retired missionaries at the Hospice who might have initiated them in this apostolate. They had their actual training on the spot, from those who preceded them, as Frederic Giroud noted in his important work: *The Mission of the Canons of Great St Bernard Abbey (1933-1952)*.

All the same Maurice Tornay was deeply grateful for the short nursing formation he had at Fribourg in 1935, in preparation for his mission in China. Was he impatient at only healing the body? Of course not. He had such a deep

59

respect for human dignity that he treated those who came to him with as much love and courtesy as St Charles Borromeo gave to his parishioners in Milan who were suffering from the plague at the end of the 16th century.

Seeing him in action one might have said, "He is like a soldier, burnt up with the desire to go to the front."[3]

The peace at Latsa

Frs Melly and Coquoz who had come to see the situation of the region in 1930, had returned to stay in 1933, and now planned to build a Hospice at the Latsa Pass, at a height of some 3800 metres. Work began on this hospice in 1935, after eighteen months of negotiations and difficulties. It had something in common with the Great St Bernard Abbey. Just like the Abbey centuries before, so now the new Hospice would offer help and succour to the thirty thousand caravan porters who used this Pass to reach the Mekong valley from Salouen and return. It would also be a place to rest and get fresh supplies.

Like the old Abbey, it had to face up to brigands and to the mortal dangers often met by the porters. Those who took the track dug by Fr Georges Andre of the FMP with pick and axe, had to spend one night in the open. It was not unusual to find their remains scattered round the Pass the following spring.

The main plans for the hospice had been drawn up in Switzerland before the departure of the missionaries. It was hoped that the hospice would also serve as an ideal refuge for any Fathers chased from their residences by the intolerance of the Lamas or by the pressures of war. The track from Weisi to the Latsa Pass is direct, as the crow flies, but it takes four days on foot or mule-back to reach it. The distance on these mountains is not counted in hours but evaluated by the number of pipes smoked or rosaries recited!

It was only possible to supervise the work, which began in summer, when the weather conditions were favourable. Often at that time the monsoons from India deluged the whole region. To reach Latsa, the Fathers' caravan would

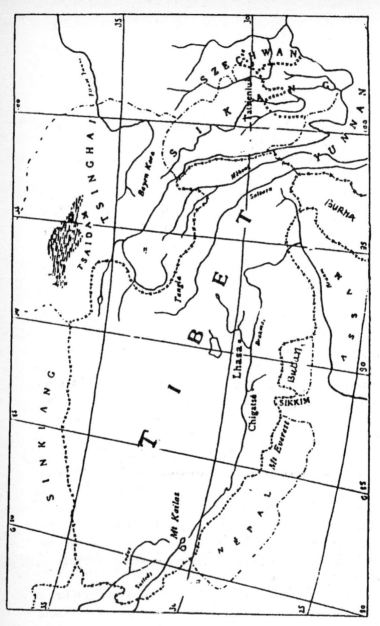

Map of Tibet and the Tibetan marshes

pass through the valley of Eternal Spring, and could encounter merchants with business on the Weisi plateau. Suddenly they might find themselves in a narrow gorge with a track like paths alongside the brooklets at Valais, hanging over emptiness or with flowing waters. Such tracks had to be followed to reach the Mekong valley.

Nothing made Maurice feel afraid for he was a true son of the mountains. The little band followed the path as far as Siao-Weisi, "a village which was almost entirely Catholic, where Fr Coquoz lived". The inhabitants were descendants of the first converts of Bonga. The path through the forests of pine and walnut were a delight after the difficulties of the journey thus far. Then they saw, with joy, fields of barley and wheat, like those at Valais. Fr Maurice recognised the crops along the terraces. If his heart then turned to thoughts of La Rosiere and Cretes, he did not allow it to linger long but came back to the present, strengthened by the certainty that he was in the prayers and thoughts of those he had left behind.

The river was always very full in summer and it had to be crossed to reach the slopes of Latsa. Bridges were almost non-existent and the safety of the cable of plaited bamboo which was generally used to cross the Mekong river appeared terribly shaky to our European travellers! Would they hesitate? Certainly not these brave mountaineers already accustomed at Great St Bernard's Abbey to the technical difficulties of such high crossings.

Maurice was linked up, lowered his head under the cable, joined his hands above the piece of wood which served as sliding-bar and was propelled to the other bank. Did he realise that several missionaries had already been drowned in crossing the river? After that, there were still eight or nine hours to walk before they would reach the Pass, which was surrounded by rhododendrons. The caravan passed Tapintze, then Kiatze where they stopped for a well-earned rest with the "besset" or chief of the village. They completed the final stage the next day, marvelling at the untouched beauty of the mountain.

When they reached Latsa, they saw a team of about hundred men from around Kiatze. They worked very slowly, partly because they were inexperienced, partly because they were not fond of hard work, and partly because of the abuse by the politicians who often commandeered men from the surrounding villages. The part of the refuge which was already built, served as shelter for the group, lodging for travellers and stables for the pack-animals. A little lower down were the foundations of the hospice. The Servant of God was thrilled to be so high, so near heaven in such a lovely place where nature itself seemed to share his search for spiritual values. There was no apparent conflict here between the visible and the invisible. Everything invited to recollection, to silence and to prayer. "I cannot walk around without praying," he wrote.

Living at 4000 metres, he was able to have a rest after the fatigue resulting from a hard-working term at Weisi. He went on with his study of Chinese, "that incomprehensible language," whilst the work on the hospice buildings continued. He sent a note to the Great St Bernard Abbey: "Dear Brothers, Here I am on the Pass where we are staying and from where I write to you with fingers frozen with cold. It is so peaceful that at the other end (of the platform) I can hear a piece of bark fall from branch to branch till it reaches the ground. The sky is exquisitely blue and the mist from the valleys rises into it silently. There is an imperceptible wind that makes green waves among the rhododendrons and bamboos. It is so beautiful! I end now, inviting you to come to see me here."

Maurice was happy. He could not have foreseen that this magnificent project to build the hospice would be abandoned in 1939 when its originator, Fr Melly was obliged by poor health, to return to Switzerland. The Second World War also cut off all contacts with Switzerland, including all remittance of money. But is not work for God "a moral task so great and beautiful in itself that the results are unimportant?" After a month of hard work during that summer of 1935, the construction was stopped until the following July.

La Rosiere, birthplace of Blessed Maurice Tornay.

Cretes, high meadows belonging to the Tornay family.

Jean Joseph Tornay, father of the Blessed.

Faustine Helene, born Rossier, mother of the Blessed.

The house where Blessed Maurice Tornay was born.

The Great St Bernard Abbey, Valais, Switzerland.

Fr Maurice Tornay before leaving for the Tibetan mission.

The three travellers, February 1936, on board the "Andre Lebon" at Marseille.
Fr Tornay is on the extreme right.

The little town of Weisi (Yunnan), China.

The Mission House at Weisi.

The first seven missionaries from the Great St Bernard Abbey at Weisi. Fr Tornay is on the extreme left in the second row.

Hanoi 24 IV 38.

Mon cher Louis,

Ton frère est prêtre depuis ce matin. Ce que nous attendions depuis 14 ans est arrivé... Je te bénis; je bénis Louise et tous vos enfants, de toute mon âme. Après demain, je dirai la Messe pour tous les miens. Toutes vos larmes, toute notre douloureuse séparation sera là sur l'autel, avec le Christ immolé; et de mes deux mains j'offrirai cela au bon Dieu pour notre salut. Non je ne sache rien de plus beau. Je suis seul, mais je suis très heureux parce qu'ainsi Dieu est davantage honoré.

After his first Mass
at Siao-Weisi,
3 July 1938.

Translation of the letter

My dear Louis,

*Your brother is a priest since this morning. What we have been
waithing for during fourteen years has happened... I bless you. I bless
Louise and all her children with all my heart. The day after tomorrow,
I will celebrate Mass for all my family. All our tears, all our painful
separations will be there, on the altar with the immolated Christ; with
my two hands I will offer all to God for our salvation.*

*No, I know nothing more beautiful. I am alone but I am happy
because thus God is more honoured.*

*The minor seminary of
Houa lo pa, seen from
Weisi.*

*Landscape of the Yerkalo
(Yen-tsing).*

Fr Tornay in his office at Houa la po, reading war news.

Fr Emile Burdin MSP in conversation with Fr Tornay who succeeded him at Yekalo in 1945.

The lamasery of Karmda which incited the persecution.

Gun Akio, civil and religious leader. A leading figure in the persecution.

Fr Tornay rests at Weisi after his expulsion from Yerkalo.

Yerkalo village (Tibet),Church, Mission house and fields.

Redemptorist Fathers' Chapel in Hanoi, where Fr Tornay was ordained.

Mr Henry de Torrente, Swiss Ambassador in Nankin, 1947-1948.

Opposite:
Atuntze town from where Fr Tornay set out for Lhasa.

Painting of Fr Tornay by Raphael Terrini, 1992.

A painting of Fr Tornay after photos, by Antonio of San Roman, 1954.

Drawing by Casimira Dabrowska, after photos, 1954.

Fr Tornay's tomb at Atuntze, 1949-1987.

Mgr. Sylvain Pierre Valentin, Bishop of Kangting after his expulsion from China.

The preparatory school

On October 1936, the Servant of God who had spent his holidays overseeing the work at Latsa, was back in Weisi. Fr Melly was the director of the Mission and Fr Lattion studied Chinese and took care of the new Preparatory School which was intended to prepare youths for the minor seminary. The Fathers hoped this would be a way of forming future priests and thereby establishing a native clergy. "Br Nestor Rouiller was the Martha of the Residence." Maurice continued with his studies and gave religion lessons to the pupils of the Preparatory School since by now he had acquired a working knowledge of the language of the country. He proved to be an excellent educator and a discerning psychologist and looked after the pupils with extreme patience and kindness. The mission itself served as a dispensary where medicines were given out, wounds dressed and epidemics checked through vaccinations. These charitable works were the basis of the evangelisation of the mission. However the greater part of their energy was spent in their work of education and instruction although many of the children had little inclination to learn. They wanted to be out looking after the flocks and tilling the land, whilst their fathers went trading from place to place along the mountain tracks and their mothers and sisters took care of the crops and the beasts. However a few dozen boys in the Preparatory School were taught and maintained by the Fathers who were buoyed up with the hope of seeing one or other of them become priests.

Strengthened by his stay in Latsa, Maurice earnestly pursued his study of dogmatic theology. However, he always took his share in the Office and prayer; and he did not allow his ascetical practices such as mortification to falter.

It was an extremely cold winter. "Lately the wolves were heard howling quite close to the mission. Sometimes they even stole the pigs." Spring approached and with it the final examinations. Maurice's superior also asked him to study Tibetan since he was destined to be head of the Preparatory School where many of the pupils spoke this language.

In the summer of 1937, the young pupils were not allowed home for the long holidays because the Fathers feared they might never return. It was therefore decided to take them a little way up-stream from Weisi, about two hours on foot, to a place called Houa lo pa.

Maurice wanted to make this summer camp as attractive as possible for the pupils so that they would not be tempted to go back. That is why he organized many games which would expand their practical aptitudes and at the same time develop their social, intellectual and spiritual life.

He still continued his important work with the pupils for he educated, nourished and clothed them, looked after their health and did not allow them to behave in the way which was congenial to their primitive way of life. Their efforts at discipline were rewarded by the happiness they felt living this summer adventure together. "We chase away our present weariness with a new one and, as always happens in this life, we tire ourselves trying to rest," Maurice wrote in the diary about this summer camp.

Fr Monbeig of the FMP, at the beginning of the century, had wanted to establish the Chartreux monks at Houa lo pa where, in 1912, he had bought a very spacious property. Unfortunately his plan was not realised and the plot was neglected. The summer camp which was set up on this very land, where the boys lived in tents, walked, ran, sang and played made it appear more cheerful. The pupils grew strong living at 2500 metres, not far from the Litipin mountain chain. Each day they improved their skills. "They did everything so well and so easily that they made us blush. … I was the foolish one. Maurice Tornay humbly said, in admiration at their ability. Fr Melly left Maurice alone with

66

his pupils at Houa lo pa, but since it was not good to be too isolated, they visited the nearby villages, and got to know the inhabitants they were received with traditional hospitality and were always asked to share tea with the people. Maurice hoped that one day he would be able to speak to them about God. As the weather became very unsettled it was impossible to live under canvas with such young boys so they all returned to Weisi in mid-August.

A number of Maurice's letters spoke of his good health and his perfect integration into the life at Yunnan, of his optimism and his good humour when faced with very novel situations. "As regards your shepherd boy, your schoolboy and your student of the past," he wrote in 1937, "he is now so acclimatised to his new life that nothing surprises him." He did not forget his family: "I can picture La Rosiere which must be growing green again. I can see the sun shining on the windows of the school and on a little corner of Cretes which looks quite black without the snow. I can hear the wind in the trees, I can smell the moss uncovered by the melting snow. I can see you at Fully hard at work on the land, and returning to La Rosiere in the evening, your hands blue with cold."

Sometimes he begged his dear family not to forget him: "I have heard nothing from you for over five months: five months make almost half a year. Imagine not to be able to find time to write in half a year! However I absolve you because I know you are good people. Go in peace, but write to me at once."

He also asked for reinforcements from the Great St Bernard Abbey "…send many missionaries out to us, but only send those who are not too elated by success and not too depressed at the lack of it."

Difficulties at Houa lo pa

The months passed peacefully, though in a land under-mined by civil war and ravaged by brigands, this peace was only the cover of a future drama. In July 1937 and 1938 the work on the Hospice at Latsa was slowed down by con-flicts, strikes and finally by a breach of contract. The work-shops would never reopen.

But the untiring Fr Melly had another project: to move the Preparatory School to Houa lo pa, on the land destined for the monks. On account of the growing number of pupils who came from as far away as Yerkalo, the buildings at Weisi had become too small to hold them all. A contract was signed with a builder and the work began in September 1937, but there were frequent delays because of the war and the menace of expropriation.

Meanwhile Maurice finished his studies and passed his examinations brilliantly in January 1838. The moment that he had been eagerly awaiting had come, the moment of his ordination. He was to climb another rung in his service of God and each step towards a greater commitment was for him a step towards greater love for his Chinese and Tibetan brothers and sisters. The priesthood was his path of perfec-tion.

On 26 March 1938, he set out with M. Chappelet for Tonkin, a journey of ten days on horseback, two days by truck and three days by train. Why did he make such a long journey for his ordination when there was a bishop of the Tibetan Mission at Tatsienlou? It was because the paths which led there were worse and less safe than those which led to French Indochina by way of the Litipin Pass.

On 5 April the travellers reached Tali, on the 9th Yuunanfou and on Good Friday, 15 April, they reached

Hanoi. How the places revisited must have awakened memories of his first journey! On 20 April, Maurice was ordained sub-deacon by Mgr Chaize, on 22 April, deacon and on Sunday 24 April he was ordained priest. His joy overflowed. He wrote to his brother Louis, "Your brother is a priest since this morning," and to his parents in La Rosiere: "Papa, Mama, your son is a priest since yesterday. Glory to God! Peace to you! Alas, you will not be too happy since you could not be here to see me. This joy and delight that you had so long awaited was taken from you just when you were going to see it realised. I have only one thing to say, I am sure you will understand for you are Christians. Here it is: We have to serve God alone with all our strength; that is why I left for the mission and why you bore my departure so bravely." It is worth underlining the sentence: "That is why I left..." He had said the same thing in different terms to Canon Gabioud just before he began his journey: "I think I have a different ideal." Young Maurice Tornay had another plan, he was called to an uncommon destiny. After his ordination he was well on the way to its realisation.

On 25 April, he said his first Mass privately at Hanoi, and on 3 July he celebrated a solemn High Mass at Siao-Weisi. That was indeed a day of thanksgiving, a time to gather all the Christians together from the region already evangelised. The new priest spoke in Chinese and had a word even for those who had come merely out of curiosity. Finally, enraptured and serious but full of happiness, he blessed the whole assembly. On his return to Weisi he continued his study of the Tibetan language and was put in charge of the Preparatory School. "How many thorns need trimming, how many brambles need uprooting! The work of the Church is indeed a great one."

It was decided to send the pupils home during the summer of 1938 whilst the work on the new site was carried on during these months when the construction work would not be interrupted by bad weather. Maurice went to Tsechung to visit Fr Georges Andre FMP and to improve his Tibetan. He studied there for a whole month, then was able to preach in this language in Patong church. He had not lost his determination to succeed nor his reliance on the grace of God!

Just when the lessons were about to begin again in the Preparatory School, brigands attacked Atuntze in the north and killed at least forty people. The population was in utter confusion and transport slowed down because the bridges, those strategic points over the rivers, had been destroyed. Fr Maurice, with the pupils from the Mekong valley, reached Weisi at long last, on 24 September. The journey had taken three weeks because of the difficulties on the road. Bands of soldiers belonging to the National Army went round the country restoring order and calming spirits, which was all that they could do.

Maurice had thirty pupils to instruct in work and in obedience. "I teach them everything, from how to wash and dress to how to kneel and pray. I am occupied with them all day, for religion has to be taught little by little, at each moment, as if I were inoculating the boys against some poison. I have a real struggle against their laziness and sometimes against my own."

In February 1939, Fr Tornay realised that the work was progressing very slowly at Houa lo pa. The Preparatory School for which he had been responsible since 1938 was so dear to him and took so much of his energy that he was drained of all interest and enthusiasm to the point of despair. He fell ill himself after nursing Fr Lattion during two whole months when the latter had typhoid fever. Br Rouiller used what little knowledge of medicine he had to cure Maurice who remained very weak for some time. Then at the end of May he became ill again because he was in too much of a hurry to get back to work.

Meanwhile, in Switzerland, in April 1939, Canon Nestor Adam his former Novice Master, was elected Abbot of the Congregation. Maurice was overjoyed. There was great rejoicing also on the school's new site which became his official residence from the beginning of June until 1945 – just the duration of the Second World War. He was also put in charge of the villages in the high valley of the Eternal Spring. Frs Nanchen and Lovey arrived just at the right moment for Fr Melly and Br Rouiller had to return to Valais because they too were ill. Fr Lattion became Superior of the mission in the place of Fr Melly, and the two newcomers started to learn Chinese.

The years 1939-1945 were times of trial and despair for the whole world. The tragic consequences of the terrible war were painfully endured by those in Yunnan as they had no contact with Switzerland and the whole region was devastated by famine and epidemics. The taxes that were mercilessly imposed and exactly drained them of all the meagre resources. Pillage and brigandage was rampant. Everyone armed themselves. At Houa lo pa, Fr Maurice had to refuse to take in more boys for he could not feed them, but all the same his doors were always open to welcome the terrified population who fled from the villages to escape massacre. His compassionate heart made him forget himself for the sake of the children and those in need. He shared his food and blankets with them and cut up his tent to make garments for them. He even sold some of his own clothes to meet the expenses of the school. He wrote: "To carry the cross means that one no longer knows which way to turn, to hope against hope and to love when nothing seems loveable." He had already told the Chinese at his first Mass at Siao Weisi that he would love them like his children.

After their sorrow at the death of Fr Nussbaum, parish priest at Yerkalo who was assassinated by the Lamas in the autumn of 1940, the Foreign Mission Society named Fr Burdin to replace him. In 1945 Father Lattion wrote, "Yerkalo is still a mission where martyrdom can crown an apostolic life." That was the case in 1940. Nine years later the brutal assassination of the Servant of God would prove the truth of these words. In 1941 the Bernardines lost Fr Nanchen who was drowned in the Mekong river.

Who could have foreseen that the spread of the missions, helped by reinforcements, would last such a short time? Day by day living conditions became so hard that it drained all their energy. Houa lo pa closed in August 1940, Fr Tornay had hoped to prepare some of the boys to enter the seminary. He was also busy in the dispensary, in administering the sacraments and burying the Christians. As a true missionary he did not allow himself to become dejected. "The more difficult the times, the more urgent is it to care for souls."[4] In any case, trials make one resilient. Fr Maurice did not know fear. Ignoring his own personal safety, he obtained supplies for the Preparatory School by going all over the country to obtain provisions for those who were dear to him. He gathered berries and bracken root and even got some food from the mission at Kitcha on the opposite bank of the Mekong. This struggle to survive was indeed necessary, but for him moral and intellectual formation of his pupils was much more important. All his strength, obtained in prayer was given to this, just as it had been in the seminary at Great St Bernard Abbey. He abandoned himself into the hands of God and his great mercy. All he did was for God's glory, out of love for his brothers and for his personal sanctification.

As the Second World War broke out in 1940 all money orders and letters from Europe to the missions were halted. The Preparatory School then developed in an unexpected way. The pupils formerly had gone for further studies to Tali or Yunnanfou when they left school, but now these institutions were obliged to refuse them as they had insufficient food for all. Fr Tornay took over the formation of his adolescents himself, first in the Junior seminary then as seminarians.

Fr Lovey caught typhoid fever at the Christmas of 1944, when visiting Fr Burdin at Yerkalo. Fr Burdin nursed him so devotedly that he recovered completely. Unfortunately Fr Burdin then contracted the fever and, exhausted by his toils, died, aged thirty-six, on 16 February 1945, just two months after he had nursed his companion to full recovery. The mission felt devastated by the departures and deaths.

Who could replace Fr Burdin at Yerkalo, a parish as

vast as the whole of France? Who would have the energy to face up to the hatred of the armed Lamas on the salt plain who would not be satisfied until the religion that was a threat to their oppressive hegemony had been completely wiped out? Fr Lovey seemed the natural choice. Yet Fr Tornay was the one chosen to continue the Planting of the Gospel in the "Land of the Spirits." What was his reaction to this decision of his superiors? It is difficult to imagine him hesitating, equivocating or defending with countless arguments the survival of the School, even though he realised his departure would mean its closure. Since his courage, his energetic temperament and his strength of character and will drove him to do only what God wanted, humbly, but with determination, he decided to accept this new challenge.

This call to a more difficult apostolate filled him with joy for he would finally enter his beloved Tibet. Nevertheless he felt immensely sad when, in April 1945, he learnt that the Preparatory School, for which he had worked so hard, was to close, as there was no one to replace him. Br Duc would stay back to look after the land and so provide revenue for the mission.

Maurice answered "Yes" to the call as he wanted to bring Christ to this strange nation and to accompany those simple people on the road to the knowledge and imitation of Christ. At this particular moment, his leadership and missionary qualities emerged fully. He was quite well aware of the risks, he knew the martyrology of Yerkalo, but he set out with enthusiasm. At the beginning of June 1945, he left Tsechung where he had been staying with Fr Gore since April to perfect his Tibetan. He went up to Yerkalo, following in the steps of the first martyrs of the parish which was founded in 1865. Right from the inception of the mission the missionaries had often had to face the anger of the Lamas who had persecuted in many ways all those who had dared to cross the frontier into forbidden Tibet and who, they suspected, would perhaps diminish their authority. The thought of Frs Bourdonnec, Vignal and Nussbaum, all martyrs of faith at the hands of the Lamas and their accomplices, rather than checking his advance urged him on. Fr Lovey came to meet Fr Tornay at Petine on his way to his new mission.

On 5 June 1945 as he reahed his new mission field, he received a very warm welcome from the people of Yerkalo. What did this respectful courtesy and enthusiastic welcome signify? Was it to gain the confidence of the unsuspecting newcomer so as to persecute him more easily later on? Fr Tornay was not naïve as to be deceived but he played their game. God ordained him to be there rather than at Houa lo pa: "The good God has always treated me better than I deserve," he wrote to his family in January 1946. He was convinced that God's grace would not fail him at such a grave moment.

Undesirable at Yerkalo

"Go and teach all nations." This command of the Lord admitted no barriers. Fr Tornay knew that Tibet was a nation dear to God although it had watered the soil with the blood of his "witnesses". Would there one day be a strong and vigorous Christian community there? He was encouraged in his plans by communications from Switzerland, finally re-established after six years silence. "For a long time I had not heard your voices..." He was at last able to write to his dear parents, to his community and to speak to them of his apostolate and to ask for their prayers and thoughts at the moment when he was being sent as a sheep among wolves. He was interested to know who was still alive at La Rosiere and who all had lately been buried in the cemetery at Orsieres. The Servant of God asked many questions but did not waste too much time over them. Yerkalo needed all his zeal and attention.

Yerkalo... the most interesting of the mission posts, the doorway to the country of the Lamas.

Yerkalo... a piercing name with little melody in it; a name which often was at the centre when something tragic like a persecution or opposition to the all-powerful lamaseries, is remembered.

Fr Tornay was well aware of all this for he listened carefully to the stories and witness of his brethren. His eyes certainly were not impervious to the beauty of the place: a plateau inclining slightly towards the deep Mekong valley which it overshadowed from 2650 metres. The snow-capped mountain tops seemed but a stone's throw away. The villages were separated by valleys and deep gorges. The glacier of Damiang sparkled on the horizon, 5000 metres high.

Yerkalo... "There is very little grass around for hardly

has it come above the ground than the sun and the wind shrivel it up. It crackles underfoot almost as if it were frozen. The many flowers are thickly woven together into sheets. There is nothing delicate about them, rather they are resistant like the edelweiss which grows in abundance. Under the blazing sun their perfume almost burns our throats."

Yerkalo... "The countryside is magnificent. Immense and infinitely white mountains, woods and tiny plains, slopes and rocks, all convey an impression of power and beauty difficult to imagine. For months it hardly ever rains but the wind blows fiercely nearly all the time. Barley and buckwheat are grown in the fields. The gardens produce potatoes, but the pear trees only bear bitter fruit." Here the poet of La Rosiere is sharing with us the magic spell of Yerkalo.

Since the climate was very dry it was particularly suitable for working the salt marshes, the main riches of the region. At the edge of the plateau where the village lies, the salt workers construct terraces of boards, leaving a space between the soil and this platform calculated to obtain the maximum amount of salt. They then draw water and send it along the terraces and when it evaporates it leaves salt behind. They next sweep the surface salt together and remove any that has been left in little stalactites round the supports of the platform. A great deal of the income of Yerkalo comes from the sale of salt, even in the distant regions of the country. Sometimes it is bartered for cereals.

If the communist advance had not brought fire and slaughter all over China, if the Lamas had not spoiled their relations with the people by material and spiritual demands almost impossible to satisfy, Tibet could have been a peaceful place instead of a place of this "loneliness which causes fear and which isolates", a loneliness the Servant of God was to experience in all its aspects.

From high in the valley of Kionglong the lamasery of Karmda can be seen, a tiny village clustered round its temple. Fr Maurice visited it. He knew that hidden behind the daily ceremonies was real despotism. "Dictators of the gods, they pretend to grant men's desires through their prayers, dances and spells." The monks who lived in that lamasery had lost the original purity of their religion just as had their leader, Gun-Akio. They did however practise healing, the education of young boys and a phantom justice. They managed with jealous care the property which was nominally that of the Dalai-lama but of which they kept the income for themselves. They were very often "sorcerers, soothsayers, and magicians who dabbled in necromancy and occultism" or else they were skilled riders and lived as marauding brigands and murderers on the highways. Since the Lamas had received the mission to honour the gods and manage the spirits that caused fear among the people, they demanded large presents in return for their intercessions from their blinded and indoctrinated followers. Although theocracy was the governmental practice of Tibet, the Lamas established a kind of dictatorship. Evangelisation could only advance by tiny steps in face of their stranglehold.

If Fr Tornay hated hypocrisy and disliked making concessions, he avoided quarrelling with the monks of Gun-Akio. He just went straight ahead in his service of God.

He loved the Christians of his parish which had already been marked by death and trials and would willingly have given his life for them so that they should not be without a priest. The people of Yerkalo were attracted to their new and fifteenth parish priest. Maurice made light of his loneliness although he was an eight-days walk away from his nearest colleague. He was responsible for about three hundred and fifty Christians who were wonderful in their fidelity to the faith, who refused to apostasize when the Lamas threatened them with all kinds of sanctions. He was determined to give himself entirely to them in spite of the double-dealing of the Gun-Akio administration. "I want to wear myself out in God's service," he had written to his brother Louis the year he left Switzerland. The moment had come to carry this out for "it is important to be ready always to begin again, in spite of and against all obstacles, without ever being discouraged. Then when death comes you have conquered it."

The difficulties the local governor had caused to his predecessors were not long in making their appearance. Fr Maurice noted in his "V" diary, dated September 1945 to January 1946, "I had hardly arrived in Yerkalo before whispers went round that the missionary should be chased away." Then in September of the same year: "In Yerkalo, the report that the missionary will definitely be sent away from Tibet is becoming much stronger. The reasons or manner of expulsion are not clearly explained. At the moment the chorus of complaints about the land has begun. Those to whom it once belonged want to regain for nothing the land their predecessors had sold for a high price." On 5 November he writes: "Whilst the Lamas of the lamasery at Kanda (Karmda) were engaged in ceremonial dancing, it was proclaimed before heaven and earth that the missionary would soon have to leave under threat of having to undergo the worst punishments that could be thought of; also that the Christians would have to apostasize and that their children would have to wear the lama toga, because there should only be one religion in the country of a thousand gods." The Christian doctrine seemed to Gun-Akio an organised, threatening force which would weaken the hegemony.

Hardly had Maurice Tornay settled at Yerkalo with Fr Lovey to help him, than Mgr Valentin asked them to visit the community at Batang without a priest for the last ten years. On 20 June 1945, when the Frs were travelling northwards on the upper reaches of the Blue River, they intercepted a telegram coming from Gun-Akio who was staying for a time in Lhasa. It was addressed to the Karmda lamasery and demanded the expulsion of the missionaries in these terms: "I will take steps so that the government will tell the English and French authorities to recall all their subjects resident in Tibet." Here was an explosive message; in any case it expressed clearly the intention to get rid of foreigners. The two Fathers understood the gravity of the situation and sent the contents of the telegram to their superiors. To the Christians at Batang, surviving in spite of the difficulties, they brought the help of the sacraments and the comfort of dialogue. They baptised, heard confessions, regularised marriages and when they had finished their mission, on 30 June, they returned to Yerkalo. They were back with their parishioners and also back into the mesh of the net cast by Gun-Akio.

Chased away like a criminal

These months before autumn were the last ones before the blood-thirsty Lama-chief Gun-Akio made his bitter attack against the brave Servant of God, Maurice Tornay. What reasons could he give? He had indeed to give a reason because he dared not declare openly that it was his hatred of the Catholic religion that prompted him. Maurice showed us the alleged motive in his journal – it was the land belonging to the mission of Yerkalo. In this country "a man belongs to the religion of the one who feeds him". It is easy then to understand what Gun-Akio was trying to do. If he got back the land he hoped to enslave once again those who occupied it and thus repulse the challenge posed by the Church in its struggle against slavery and social injustice.

The person using the land had a status which differed according to the one who owned it. Nearly all land belonged to the lamaseries, and thus to the religious and political leaders and to a few highly privileged individuals. It had been a vitally important step for the former missionaries to acquire some property where they hoped to establish Christian farmers. They thought they would free them from the feudal dues paid to the lamaseries. What did buying and selling signify for the people? The word has not the same connotation when it is pronounced in Yerkalo or in Orsieres. Land that had been "sold" could be taken back by its former owner: selling was thus a loan on a more or less long term basis.

This meant that the mission was very insecure and found it difficult to claim its rights and, still more, to carry out its plans of evangelisation. Happily, in the past, the Lhasa government had come to its defence, but the Lamas still had other weapons. They took their revenge on the Christians, expelled the American pastors, then killed others, including Fr Nussbaum and tried to poison Fr Burdin who had both been former parish priests at Yerkalo. To wipe out the Catholic religion was it not necessary first to get rid of its ministers? "The Lamas want to kill Fr Maurice and will not rest until they have destroyed Christianity in Tibet," Fr Lovey wrote to Mgr Adam.

After Fr Burdin's death and with the arrival of Maurice, came a change of tactics. Following an alleged order from Lhasa, Gun-Akio said that he had to take a census of men and animals. Before this, he ordered ceremonies to be held which included intercessory prayers to the gods. He hoped to impress his subjects and to demand dues from them. He made no exceptions and if the Christians did not follow his demands the Chief-Lama would order them to repair the roads and bridges. These threats were in reality, an attack on the Fathers. Gun-Akio wove a web of intrigues; he would drive them from their land together with the Christians if they did not restore their possessions immediately to their former owner, an apostate Christian, so that he could then reclaim them for himself; or he would ask the Christians of Yerkalo to pay a big fine for having ground their grain at the mission mill; he also continued to utter various threats of expulsion either against the missionaries or against the Christians.

Such was the situation at Yerkalo. The Father was well integrated in his new parish and made no effort to seek a compromise. Justice remained his guiding rule.

He would never give in to Gun-Akio's blackmail. "He sought the absolute," the absolute would lead him to the heroism of total sacrifice. Fr Lovey had returned to his apostolate in Tsechung at the end of August 1945, so Maurice remained the only one responsible for the Christians. The fact that Fr Tornay was Swiss seemed to offer to Gun-Akio and the Lamas an additional hold on him. They declared: "We sold our land to the French and not to the Swiss. Thus we have the right to reclaim it." Fr Tornay resisted them. "Here I am. Here I stay." Gun-Akio became even more wily and alternated between acting as a peacemaker and a dictator. He planned things carefully, suggesting that there might be reprisals from the Chinese. They might want to get back the salt marshes seized by Tibet in 1932, now that the Japanese menace had been lifted.

At the end of the summer, all those who had formerly owned mission land banded together to reclaim their property; here again Gun-Akio was acting through intermediaries for his own advantage. Fr Tornay did not give in to their demands as he knew he was acting within his rights, for the land had been bought when Yerkalo was under Chinese rule. "The French missionaries will have the right to hire or buy land in any of the Provinces and may build churches and houses there," stated Chinese law. Thus the Yerkalo land was bought in perpetuity, "in conformity with the acquisition norms of land ownership according to Chinese law. The animosity of the Lamas became ever more fierce. In October 1945, the Chief-Lama sent Ramti, his delegate, with orders that Fr Maurice should go to Tsekou, near Tsechung, leaving everything he possessed behind. His own superiors advised him not to give in to anything but violence.

In November 1945, came another attempt. The stewards of Karmda visited the mission to harvest the remaining cereals, and ordered Fr Maurice to get out. He replied, "I will only leave if you compel me by force." The time-limit passed. Then Gun-Akio renewed his threats and, trying to get help at the highest level, sent new calumnies to the Governor of Chando. Maurice remained resolutely determined. During the final months of that year he suffered from incessant threats, vexations and also continual postponements of his departure. Finally, on 9 January 1946, Gun-Akio appeared in person. "We want no more Christians here," he said. And Fr Maurice answered, "My superiors have forbidden me to leave my post." On 13 January he added: "I will only go if the Lamas bind me to a beast." His parishioners were in despair but supported him bravely although they had found it hard, when they renounced the religion of the Lamas, to be treated as traitors to their country.

Besides asking for help from the international diplomats in Lhasa, Maurice planned to regularise his situation by going to Chamdo, the main town of the eastern province of Tibet where the Governor's residence was situated. Gun-Akio opposed this step fiercely and Maurice, as immovable and as firmly convinced of his rights as ever, met him once more. On 21 January the Lamas attacked. "Suddenly fighting, shooting, the cries of maddened men filled the air. I had hardly the time to get up when I saw thirty guns levelled at me... too bitter to embrace!" "Father, are you leaving or not?" "You must tie me up as was agreed." The residence was pillaged but finally the benevolent hypocrite, Gun-Akio, changed his mind once more. He ordered the Lamas to leave the site and gave Fr a further delay of five days.

This was at dawn, 26 January 1946. Maurice then celebrated Mass. He was "without support and yet supported", for God certainly had not completely abandoned him. His greatest regret was for his dear faithful who crowded into the chapel like children about to lose their father. He was worn out, humiliated, "frozen and stiff with sorrow". He cried to heaven for help as he was torn from his parish, "Give me light so that I may go towards an unknown land in security." His answer was: "Go forth in the darkness and put your hand in the hand of God."[5]

Gun-Akio sent twelve armed soldiers to remove him and so Fr Maurice departed, carrying nothing, armed only with his courage and with God's grace. He handed over to his Christians the possessions of the mission securely locked in boxes and gave them the winter cereals. He placed seals on the doors to show that he left nothing to his enemies. Sorrowfully he bade his Christians farewell.

He set out towards Petine, with a gun at his neck. The soldiers took him as far as Pame and he went with head held high. He had lived through his greatest sorrow, that of being separated from his Christians. He prayed. He had already had a premonition that his life would be short. What he had sown on the rocks of Yerkalo, all the same, one day, perhaps, would come to fruition.

He stopped at Pame but the Lamas threatened him again because they considered that he was still too close to the Tibetan frontier. Whilst in that village a messenger arrived from the Governor at Chamdo with a promise to re-install him in his mission. Maurice began to hope that the situation was not as desperate as he had first thought. Caravans passed coming from Yerkalo and brought the news that his Christians were more united than ever because of the trials they were experiencing. Those who returned to Yerkalo nourished the expectations of the village that they would see their priest back with them once more.

The Governor's promise that he could return roused real but false hope, as when the messenger was going back to Chamdo, he was bribed and abandoned Fr Tornay without giving him the details of the Governor's plans to assist him. One more betrayal!

Fr Maurice went on to Atuntze and Tsechung where he sought the advice of his superiors. Another glimmer of hope. This time, the Governor invited him to return under his protection. Maurice did not need to be told twice. On 6 May 1946, he joined a caravan of Christians who were going up the Mekong valley as far as Yerkalo. He showed tenacity and courage in returning for he gained no advantage for himself, he was only seeking the good of his Christians.

Gun-Akio who was obsequious to the powerful but a tyrant with the weak, had spies who were rapid and efficient. Fr Maurice presented his permit from Chamdo but it proved useless because his return to the Mission was forbidden. When he reached Petine he was in a state of complete exhaustion.

Gun-Akio who was neither compassionate nor human, took him back himself as far as the frontier during the night saying, "It is the people who do not want either strangers or

Christians in Tibet. I can do nothing." He was a liar, and caused a great deal of trouble. *Kyrie eleison. Christe eleison.*

"Rescue me from my enemies, O my God.
Be my tower of strength against all who attack me.
Rescue me from these evildoers.
Deliver me from these men of blood.
Savage men lie in wait for me,
They lie in ambush, ready to assail me;
For no fault or guilt of mine, O Lord,
Innocent as I am, they run to take arms against me.
Arouse thyself and come to my help."

Psalm of David, No. 59.

In exile at Pame and at Atuntze

Henceforth Fr Tornay's will was intent on only one thing; to return to his faithful, who, he learnt, used to gather secretly in a hut to pray together. "I will go back to Yerkalo whatever this may cost. My faithful are being persecuted there. My duty is clear. Rather death than to leave my Christians in such a state."

In Pame where he settled once again, his apostolate was limited as there were only two Christian families. However it had the advantage of being quite near his parish so he was able to keep in contact with his parishioners and hoped to be able to rejoin them as soon as possible. It seemed clear that the persecutions endured by the missionaries could not take away the growing desire for conversion among the people. After these grave incidents there came a little calm. "Was it worth coming so far to do so little"? Fr Tornay asked himself.

During the "difficult year" between his expulsion and winter 1947, Maurice had many reasons for discouragement but he overcame them and, through his letters, organised a campaign of prayers that he might return to his poor, humiliated parish. From the depths of his great solitude he stretched forth his hands to his absent ones whose fervour and fidelity supported him.

Once again he was threatened because he had settled too close to the border. The Lamas had already taken possession of the Mission House at Yerkalo and forced the Christians to apostasize, making each family offer one son to the lamasery. Everything they did revealed that they would not hesitate to pursue him even beyond Pame.

In February 1947, some welcome reinforcements, Fathers Emery, Savioz, Fournier and Detry, arrived in Weisi where Fr Tornay was able to join them. He had been staying with Fr Lovey in the friendly oasis of Tsechung to regain his strength.

It was in 1947 that he envisaged for the first time the bold step of going to Lhasa to get what neither the consular authorities nor his superiors had been able to obtain from the Tibetan government: namely, the right to return to Yerkalo with an edict of religious freedom for his Christians, a freedom that was admitted in principle but nonexistent in practice. With Fr Lattion's approval, he tried several other approaches when in Weisi. He showed the same tenacity as Fr Renou and Fr Dubernard of the FMP, his predecessors on the road to martyrdom. A photo of this period shows his face already marked by intense suffering. He seems to bear the weight of the cross on his shoulders as if caused by the premonition that "he would die kneeling, unknown and ridiculed on a dark village night, surrounded on every side by savage men". But he was strengthened in his determination by the examples of the many priests who had given their lives whilst exercising their apostolate.

During the winter 1947-48, Fr Tornay went up to Atuntze a Sino-Tibetan commercial centre of some importance, as it was also a frontier post with a garrison. He obeyed the decision of his superiors with courage and prudence. He settled down in this long-established parish, and had the joy of meeting Christians from Yerkalo who traded in the Mekong valley. He cared for the sick and since the Mission House was falling into ruin, he decided to restore it. This work prevented him from sinking into discouragement and depression. He did as much good as he could in the village without having the consolation of seeing many conversions, for reasons that can be readily understood.

He wrote to La Rosiere and to the St Bernard Hospice to seek spiritual and financial help, in order to realise his projects. At the Mother House at that time, unfortunately, they were little able to help the missions. Maurice suffered, but realised that the increase in the number of young men in formation meant much greater expenses for the hospice.

He was happy that the parishes of Valais, in spite of their own needs, were able to help him.

Then at Atuntze the unexpected happened. He was sent to Kunming, the episcopal residence of Mgr Derouineau, as Fr Gore's delegate. He had to explain to Mgr Riberi, the Nuncio to China, what had happened in Yerkalo. However, Mgr Riberi could not leave Nankin because of the revolution. What did that matter! Fr Tornay would himself travel to Nankin to met him. Distances counted for nothing before the priority of the Mission and his desire to find a successful solution. Mgr Derouineau decided to finance his journey by air. On 21 February 1948, Fr Maurice was in Shangai and attended the closing ceremony of an assembly of delegates from Christian Schools. He went on to Nankin where he saw the Nuncio on 3 March. The Nuncio learnt of the desperate situation at Yerkalo and, seeing Maurice's determination, advised him to go to Lhasa as planned to get the guarantees he needed; in fact he told him that it was his duty to do so.

He offered him 200 American dollars to cover some of his expenses. Profiting of his stay in Nankin, Maurice also visited M.H. e Torrente, the Swiss minister in China who was full of promises, then the French Ambassador and finally members of the Tibetan Pomda family which was very influential. Wherever he went he was encouraged to go to Lhasa. He also obtained medical supplies for Atuntze, and he hoped for Yerkalo as well. He had wasted neither his time nor his money!

He then returned to Kunming (Yunnanfou) where, on 25 March, he learnt that his beloved mother had died. He was overcome thinking how she had longed to see her son and missionary at least once again before her death. He who loved her tenderly and venerated her as a saint had not been with her when she crossed the threshold into eternal happiness. Although Maurice was heart-broken, quickly he pulled himself together for he realised that every separation forges another bond.

On 11 June 1948, he returned to Atuntze and continued

his evangelical and humanitarian work for those he loved. The sick people he cured were recalled immediately to the Lama's territory. Fr Tornay remained hopeful and also followed with great interest the re-organisation of the mission of the Great St Bernard which was considering a separation from the FMP in order to become autonomous. This would make for greater efficiency, especially in cases like the one which preoccupied him.

From the summer of 1948 Maurice thought more and more of his great project though he said little. Yet each time a caravan passed, going towards Lhasa, he would sigh and say, "How I would like to be going too." Meanwhile, he built up the mission house which had been falling into ruins and acted both as carpenter and roofer. He arranged a small chapel, and dreamt of establishing a leper hospital and, with this in mind, only spent what was strictly necessary. It seemed as if there was not enough time to organise everything before he would have to leave. Winter passed. On 17 February 1949, a caravan was attacked by bandits after it had left the village and ten muleteers and merchants were killed. This was a mean revenge because the brigands had lost some men when the frontier guards had challenged them. "At present, here there are people who feel obliged to kill just as others feel the need to eat."

When Fr Savioz came to Atuntze to learn Tibetan, Maurice felt he might be able to get away. Since he was attracted to the hardest path and to the absolute and was not inclined either to the easy way or to giving up his purpose, Maurice prepared for the difficult road ahead. His ardent wish to return to his parishioners at Yerkalo remained unchanged

He was anxious to undertake the arduous journey to Lhasa, a project inexplicable in purely human terms. "I must get ready for the journey," he wrote to his friend, Fr Lovey in May 1949. Do not be deceived. He was not impatiently trying to settle the conflict, nor was he led by ill-regulated ardour. He would take no unnecessary risks, but had carefully worked out the whole plan. Both Mgr

Derouineau and the Nuncio had encouraged him to pursue his project and he felt his duty lay there. He also remembered that Lhasa had strongly defended the mission on several occasions.

Because he hated compromise and always made straight for his goal, he felt compelled to take this heroic path. Did not God himself want him in Yerkalo? He was always extremely careful to follow the inspirations of grace. "The determination he showed did not come from obstinacy. Some causes call for the complete gift of self. The cause of Christ is such and requires intrepid defenders and witnesses." Who can say in what degree heroism is a result of the human will and in what degree a result of divine grace? There is a true symbiosis between the disciple and his Master.

Maurice understood clearly the risks he would face. When they had expelled him from Yerkalo, the Lamas did not hide the fact that they wanted to kill him and they had attacked him as soon as he had returned there in 1946.

Now that Japan had been conquered the struggle between the communists and the Nationalist troops had resumed more fiercely than ever and brigands used the state of anarchy to get rich at the expense of the people. Fr Tornay wrote once more to his friend Fr Lovey who was in Tsechung: "There is no need to ecomomise as we will certainly be pillaged from top to bottom. I ask for your prayers as it will take a lot of courage and ability to undertake the journey." But his mind was completely made up. Fr Lattion, his superior, and Fr Gore, the Vicar-General of the Bishop of Kanting for the Tibetan Marches, still had to authorise his departure. Maurice wrote his last letters. "The worst thing is to do nothing." Since the diplomatic channels acted so slowly, he chose the journey to Lhasa to try to obtain his return to Yerkalo. If his mission failed, he hoped to be expelled to India so that he might approach the British authorities there. Above all he wanted his plan to remain secret.

90

His last weeks

In June 1949, the Servant of God learnt that a caravan of Christian merchants was about to leave Tsechung for Lhasa, passing through Atuntze and loaded with tea, oil and flour. There remained just a few weeks for him to obtain leave from his superiors to set out, and to arrange his expedition down to the smallest details. He even decided what arms he would take to ensure the protection of his companions and the pack animals when they returned. "How far will I get? What will happen? I promise nothing." On 10 July 1949, Fr Tornay celebrated Mass quietly at dawn so as to avoid spreading news of his departure. No-one knew of his project except Frs Savioz, Lattion and Gore and the members of the caravan, including his faithful servant, Doci, who had been with him since he was chased from Yerkalo.

He distrusted the tricks of Gun-Akio and wanted to avoid the possibility of being spied on, so he went southwards and then the caravan took the normal track to the north. Fr Savioz went a little way with him. Doci was one of the travellers and never left his master's side. "A vague presentiment weighed on our hearts," noted Fr Savioz in his diary. Then came the sad moment of separation. Each went on his way, Fr Savioz went up the Dong valley towards the Djroula pass whilst Maurice and Doci rejoined the caravan that very evening.

Their caravan, led by Steouang, was joined by another coming from Chedi, which included friends of the caravan leader. There were twenty-five people in all. They went down towards the Mekong crossing. On the backs of their mules, Maurice and his helpers had packed wheat, medicines, food, clothing, necessities for the journey and all that was needed to celebrate Mass. They had also loaded useful objects such as watches, binoculars, money, gifts, a machine gun and a revolver. Steouang checked everything before they left. Great prudence was needed for Fr Maurice was spied upon and threatened wherever he went and whatever he did. He certainly did not want to be caught this time. There were thirty-four stages to travel before Lhasa was reached, so nothing could be left to chance. The men walked quietly and pushed their animals before them.

Instead of following the left bank of the Mekong as they would normally have done if they were rejoining Yerkalo, they crossed the river. The track climbed up to 5000 metres on the spurs of Choula where the air was difficult to breathe. They overlooked the Salouen basin which was also part of "the roof of the world". From then on they were in Tibet.

When they reached Dialan, Fr Maurice disguised himself as a Tibetan merchant just as Fr Renou of the FMP had done in the 19th century. He shaved his goatee beard, and put on baggy trousers, long kurta, boots and belt. This was to avoid arousing suspicions at the customs since to be seen as a foreigner might compromise the safety of the caravan. He knew that Lamas told of his move, would attack him for they were afraid of his direct approach to Lhasa. They feared lest his chances with the highest authorities or even with the Dalai-Lama himself might lessen their influence.

The road they followed was a very ancient route which went up by the River Ou-khio, a tributary of the Salouen, towards Tunto. "It came from afar, from central China, entered Tibet near Lhasa and from there wound towards Sikkim and India. It seemed endless. We were very high up the mountain."[6] The different stages and the passes were marked by "chorten", little towers made of a cube, a sphere and a cone placed one on the other, symbolising that Buddha was omnipresent. Many "mani" lined the countryside. These were stones with invocations engraved on them such as: "*O mani padme oum*", which means: "Oh, may I achieve perfection and be absorbed by Buddha. Amen." Fr Maurice was drawing nearer to the holy city he so desired to reach. All around him breathed the wisdom of Buddha and here he was, just a humble priest, led by the dream of rejoining a mere handful of Christians at Yerkalo.

Very discreetly, each morning he celebrated Mass. As he walked he said the rosary and prayed that God might keep his hope alive. He shared meals with the caravan travellers, spoke with them, helped them to load and unload the mules and was well liked by them all. In the evening they camped, had a meal and kept watch by the fires. Fr Tornay gathered the Christians in his tent for evening prayer, a tent which recalled the "Tent of Meeting" between God and Israel when the Jewish people wandered through the desert. He had made friends with some of the travellers, Steouang the caravan leader, Sondjrou his brother-in-law, Jouang, another of Maurice's servants, the muleteers and the merchants. All knew his identity, all agreed to assist him should he be in trouble.

At Tchrayul, seat of the local governor, the Tomapun, and also the customs post, Steouang paid the entry fees on the loads and animals and offered a gift to the chief. Doci and his master only rejoined the caravan once the control was over and after night had fallen and they set out first the next morning. They left the party when a difficult situation arose and returned only when it seemed safe again. At Lenda they took a secondary track which crossed rich pasture land where the animals could graze. Nobody guessed that at that very moment, on the main road, Agyie and Yutun, representatives from the lamasery of Karmda were galloping along with two soldiers, one being a customs officer sent by the Tomapun at Tchrayul. They went fast, making for the lamasery of Tunto, with the papers needed for the Father's arrest. In order to act more efficaciously, they asked for help from the Lamas and the local people. The next morning, 27 July, the caravan finally reached Tunto on the seventeenth stage of their journey and they were ordered to stop. It seems probable that nobody will ever know how Karmda had been informed that Fr Maurice was travelling with this caravan.

It is possible that a certain Atun was the traitor. He left

for Tibet the same week as did the caravan led by Steouang. It might also have been Doci's fiancee who had been told confidentially of Fr Tornay's departure and could have spoken of it. Whoever it was, the Lamas thus informed "decided they had to finish once and for all, with this intruder, the missionary and man of God". They sent Agyie and Yutun to Tchrayul to stop the caravan: another messenger went up towards Chamdo, whilst four Lamas who had been promised a thousand rupees and all the booty from the caravan if they killed the Father, waited in ambush for their return.

Let us go back to Tunto. Had the Lamas thought that the Servant of God would be unsuccessful in his appeal to the authorities in Lhasa they would have left him free to travel, for his failure would have increased their prestige. However, they arrested him together with the people of the caravan and accused the leader, Steouang, of having introduced a foreigner on to Tibetan soil. The men were disarmed and ordered to retrace their steps. There was a great deal of discussion and the merchants from Chedi argued that they had not chosen the company of the Father and demanded that their weapons be returned. They were only allowed to continue when they handed over their load of tea and sent Steouang on with Maurice's caravan. Agyie and Yutun said they were acting under orders from the Lamas. The Father said, "We are trapped. We must rely on the grace of God." He apologised to the merchants for the trouble he had caused them and promised to restore the ninety sacks of tea given to the governor as compensation.

All this time, the bad news was travelling through the valleys and the passes. At Yerkalo the Christians heard that their parish priest was in trouble in the Oukhio valley and sent to inform Fr Gore. Ominously the letter was delayed on the way. Fr Savioz at Atuntze was told and tried to find reinforcements. However, nothing seemed able "to stop the course of injustice and crime".

At Tunto, in exchange for a sum of money, Fr Maurice managed to arrange that Steouang should continue as leader

94

of the caravan but the messengers from Karmda held Sondjrou, his brother-in-law, as substitute to conform with the laws. He accepted and entrusted his load to Tome, a muleteer who was going on to Lhasa and who, although he was not one of his servants, also agreed to take the tea belonging to the Father on his animals. The next day they separated. Fr Maurice wished them a safe journey and asked them to pray for him. "Lord, come and break the chains of the captives seated in darkness and in the shadow of death."

With his group went the servants Doci and Jouang, led by Sondjrou, and the five pack animals. Steouang accompanied them a little way for the messengers had not returned his precious gun and without it he would be unable to defend himself if attacked. He managed to persuade them and got his rifle back in exchange for another gift. He then returned to his group.

The soldiers with their prisoners redescended the Oukhio valley. Fr Tornay was faithful to his daily celebration of Mass and to reciting his breviary. He did not give the impression that he feared for his life. Doubtless he was excessively very distressed but regretted, mainly, the trouble he had caused the others and the lack of progress he had made for his "cause".

They travelled several more of the stages as far as Tchrayul where the local governor refused "with a chilly courtesy" any concessions and forbade the Father to take the road to Lhasa. Maurice said to him: "Steouang had nothing to do with this matter. Sondjrou, whom you see here, has come as his substitute. I ask you not to harm him. If you desire to punish somebody physically or with a fine, then punish me." However, the governor did not wish to harm them. Maurice never thought of himself, he was already wondering how he could settle the "affair" on Steouang's return. To show his good intentions the Tomapun gave him a soldier to protect him in exchange for a mule and some tea! "He felt disgust rather than fear. The path he would take at dawn, would never lead him to Atuntze where Fr Savioz was waiting for him. There seemed no further question of reaching Yerkalo. He would never see Yerkalo again."[7] The caravan set out. Fr Maurice had got his gun back but Agyie and Yutun were uneasy and so the customs officer took charge of it. Sondjrou was worried about what would happen to the caravan on its return from Lhasa. He had understood from the Chief that Steouang would have to defend himself against serious charges. Thanks to the Servant of God he was able to send Steouang a message warning him to be on his guard.

When they reached Oya, a woman begged to follow them as she was ill and wanted medical attention from the Father when they reached Atuntze. At Pitou, situated below Tchrayul, two soldiers sent by the Karmda lamasery joined them. Their mission was to take the Father back to his Tibetan mission and they had come to escort him like a common criminal. He refused to follow them and preferred to return to the Tomapun. He knew very well that since it was the Lamas who had chased him from Yerkalo, they only wanted him in order to kill him. There seemed no other reason to send such well-armed soldiers to escort him. During the night spent at Pitou, the sick woman overheard the soldiers saying that they had decided to spare Fr Maurice but would kill Doci. The following day, before they reached Dialang she told the servant what she had heard. Jouang and Sondjrou suggested to the Father that they should seize the opportunity of the halt the next day to flee towards Karbo Tchrana, from where they could follow either the Salouen or the Mekong valleys. Doci, who was unarmed, did not agree with this plan. Fr Maurice was convinced that if someone had to die it should be he and not Doci. Like heroes and saints he had the habit of always choosing the most difficult part for himself.

On 10 August, a day of rest, some of the villagers came to ask Fr Maurice for medical help. Since Agyie had to cash some money in a village in the Salouen valley, he left the soldiers guarding the prisoners. The Servant of God said several times that he was in the same situation as Fr

Nussbaum had been, and if he had to die it would be wonderful. This was made very clear when Sondjrou testified for the Process at Sikkim.

At midday, Doci was allowed to try out the machine gun which had been returned to him and then they went on to K'iobe where they prepared the camp for the night. At that moment Yutun and Agyie came rushing back: "You old beggar, who were you trying to frighten when you fired a shot at midday?" shouted Agyie. He threatened Doci with his loaded gun, knocked him down and seized the machine gun from him. Fr Maurice intervened, blessed Doci and pushed himself forward saying: "Do not fire at Doci, shoot me." To show their goodwill towards him, however, the two messengers from Karmda burnt incense and offered to give all their pistols and other arms to the soldier from Tomapun. Fr Maurice showed them no hatred nor did he resist their changing moods. He was but "the crucified parish priest from Yerklo, rejected in Tibet and chased away by force to Yunnan in China."[8]

Another day dawned. The Servant of God felt more and more strongly that there was no escape from death. He asked his servants: "Yesterday were you afraid? Do not fear, for if we are killed we will go straight to Paradise. We are going to die for the Christians." He prayed using his breviary, or said his rosary which he held firmly clasped in his hands. He had hoped, he had begged for God's help; he thought once more of the faces of his loved ones in Switzerland and those of his brethren in China; how much longer had he to hold out? Before he undertook the journey to Lhasa he had written to Fr Lovey: "Reasonable means do not seem to have achieved anything, perhaps the fools will succeed." They would not succeed either for Maurice had embraced the folly of the Cross.

The final sacrifice

Scarcely had he finished his prayers that night, "O night of Gethsemane" than the Servant of God wanted to continue the journey. He took hardly any food. He walked on foot and lent his stick to Sondjrou whom he saw was walking with difficulty. The Choula pass was in sight and then they were through it. Below lay the territory of Yunnan and China. Perhaps they would escape the wolves... They had to regain the Mekong Valley. The slope was extremely steep and the men went behind the animals. Jouang and Sondjrou led the caravan, next came Doci and Fr Maurice, then Agyie and Yutun, the soldier from Tomapun, the woman, the servant with a horse, and finally the soldier on duty with three horses closed the little procession.

Suddenly, at a place called Thotong, very suitable for an ambush, four armed Lamas burst out from the undergrowth. "So you have deigned to appear," they called and immediately began to shoot. "Do not fire," cried Fr Tornays, but already Doci, who was plainly carrying an unloaded weapon, was hit. He collapsed and fell and Maurice, kneeling beside him gave him absolution, without even trying to protect himself. Then he himself slumped to the ground under a hail of bullets.

"Thus Lord, your Servant has reached the climax of the journey that led him to you. This is my hour, Lord, the one you allowed me to meet, on this 11th day of August 1949, one marked with your sign from the beginning."

The first two caravan leaders escaped from the fusillade by leaping down the embankment, terrified by the shots the murderers fired after them. Thus did the Lamas take revenge for the genuine goodness Fr Maurice had always shown to them. No one else was killed. As Jouang and

Sondjrou had hidden in the forest they too were unharmed. "Things fell out badly today," said Jouang and began to weep. Together they went down to the village of Merechu to rouse everyone. They learnt that the four Lamas had been wandering around the village, waiting for the arrival of Fr Tornay in order to kill him. The inhabitants had asked these intimidating "unknowns", not to create trouble on their land. It was for this reason that the Lamas from Karmda lay in ambush higher up near Choula. However, the servants were not reassured. They left Merechu and on the banks of the Mekong they met people who were trying to find out when Fr Tornay's caravan was due. They got rid of them and continued towards Dong and Atuntze. The people everywhere had noticed the comings and goings of the messengers and soldiers, eleven men in all, sent from the Karmda lamasery in search of Maurice to achieve their deadly purpose.

On 12 August, Jouang and Sondjrou reached Atuntze, where the murderers would have come to find the Servant of God had he not left for Lhasa, and went immediately to Fr Savioz.

They found him desperate at the bad news that was being circulated and they told him all that had happened at Thotong. Frs Lovey and Gore in Tsechung were also informed immediately. Fr Savioz sent seven porters to the place of the ambush to bring back the bodies of the two martyrs. They found them, stripped of their clothes, but intact, lying by the roadside. Doci who had been killed by bullets also had a sabre wound on his shoulder. Fr Tornay had been shot in the temple and stomach. None of their possessions were to be found.

On 16 August, when the porters returned, Sondjrou and Jouang lovingly washed and prepared the bodies of Maurice and Doci. Fr Lovey, his dearly beloved, arrived the evening of the 17th. The two martyrs were already buried in the garden of the Mission House, so he did not have the consolation of seeing for the last time the face of his brother and friend from La Rosiere.

Sadly those who had known and loved Maurice sought the reason for the brevity of his life. But who can understand the designs of God for his young Servant? It was indeed hard to accept that God had allowed his death just when the mission had such urgent need of his apostolate. "If the stem bears flowers for too long, the fruit cannot ripen before the cold and death approach," Maurice had written to Anna, his sister, just before he left for China.

Complaints were made to the authorities of Yunnan and protests to the Karmda lamasery which had ordered these crimes. It all bore little weight in the face of the hatred shown for the rival religion and before the fears of fanatical men that they would lose prestige and influence or even before the pretext they made of pushing the Chinese as far back as possible to delay the advance of the Maoists.

"Tornay massacred. Lattion." read the telegram, sent on 21 September 1949, to Mgr Adam, Abbot of the Great St Bernard Abbey, who heard the sad news immediately after Mgr Derouineau, Archbishop of Kumming and Mgr Valentin, Bishop of Kanting.

The grief felt by everyone was immense. On 26 September, a funeral service was held in the church at Orsieres. The time for actions and words was over. Now was the time for the family, friends, the Congregation and all the people of Valais to mourn. They were also filled with hope at the thought of having offered a martyr to God who had not refused to his Servant his most cherished wish, that of becoming a witness and a saint. He had kept him faithful to his duty and lovingly attached to his Christians. He had enlightened his human prudence with the gift of the Holy Spirit. He kept him totally, for himself.

"One sows,
another reaps"

Was everything finished in Yunnan? Was the death of Fr Tornay going to threaten the hopes, kill the plans and stop the evangelisation of these hostile regions? Had Maurice, like so many others, died in vain? To think this is to ignore that the blood of the martyrs penetrates the soil where it is shed and renders it fruitful. Even if, in appearance, the efforts of the mission seemed useless, their results negligible and their failure almost total, those who have sown must be trusted. On 29 November 1949, a group of young Canons left Great St Bernard Abbey to carry on the work thus interrupted. Unhappily, they never reached the salt marshes: the whole of Yunnan was invaded and, from Saigon, the Swiss Consul advised the three newcomers to return to Europe.

All those who knew Fr Tornay, said, "The Father offered his life for the Christians of Yerkalo." They never suggested theft or vengeance or any other human motive as the reason for his death. Even the Fathers were astonished that the Servant of God had been able to resist the attacks of the Lamas so long. Imprudence is never spoken of, but his foresight and zeal, his obedience to his conscience and to his superiors, his fierce will to make justice and truth triumph, and finally in the service of his cause, the dangers of his journey to Lhasa, are all mentioned.

Fr Maurice was well-disposed towards martyrdom and desired it greatly not because he wanted personal renown but, like John of the Cross, he sought the glory of God alone. He felt confirmed in his most decisive undertakings by the certainty of saving his soul and the souls of his Christians.

His life and death manifest clearly that he was a witness and a martyr for it was through sheer hatred of the Faith that the Lamas pursued and finally killed him. He accepted his violent death and died forgiving his murderers.

Neither at Yerkalo nor at Karmda were the murderers arrested. They were only ordered to return Doci's gun to his father. The lamasery was fined heavily by the Chinese communists, but this was a way of keeping the esteem of the governors and remaining credible in their own eyes.

Immediately after the death of the Servant of God, events moved swiftly. The three valleys of the Blue River, the Mekong and the Salouen formed three lines of communist infiltration. There was trouble and devastation in Weisi, Kitcha and Siao-Weisi. The communist troops came from the north-east and used the salt marshes as a ladder by which they could annex Tibet and then, hopefully, continue into India. The soldiers in the three valleys took up arms to defend themselves, but it was an unequal battle. The waves of Chinese soldiers overcame them easily and the rest of the country struggled on alone to repulse them. An unprecedented barbarism followed. The starving populations were the prey to destruction, arson and pillage; they saw their cultural and spiritual values overthrown. In the general chaos it was difficult to distinguish who was opposing whom. Mao retorted to the Dalai-Lama and established everywhere a harsh revolutionary rule. Was that preferable to chaos? At first it was thought so and even the Fathers on the missions imagined a time of "liberty" had come. This was all part of the communist plan to show religious tolerance to begin with and thus allay suspicion so that later they could spread the Marxist doctrine more easily. People were soon undeceived.

Since the post was censured, the Fathers at the Great St Bernard Abbey were a long time without news of their brethren in China. These latter did all they could to ward off the innumerable dangers that threatened them, especially during the pillages, but were content that at least their lives were spared.

In November 1951, some fifteen months after the death of the Servant of God, the French and Swiss Fathers, victims of Peking's campaign against the missions, were forced to regroup at Weisi. They had been chased from their parishes, accused by the communists of being, "exploiters of the peasants and of the working class".[9] Now they were being punished as land owners just as before, they had been hated by the Lamas as propagators of the Christian faith. Pressure was exercised on the people to stop them from visiting the Fathers who had become suspect. The group was transferred first to Kunming, then to the British colony of Hong-Kong. Since they had been expelled and deprived of the right to exercise their apostolate, they asked for visas for Sikkim in India, but these were refused them. However, the Spirit was active and another pleasing land was offered them in 1952: Formosa, where the bishop of Taipeh invited them to work in his diocese. But they remained henceforth without news from the three valleys which they all felt remained "theirs".

At Valais, that same year, Mgr Adam, who had been consecrated Bishop of Sion, started the ordinary Process for the cause of Maurice Tornay. Fr Lovey, elected by the General Chapter to succeed him as Abbot of the Great St Bernard, returned from Taiwan. From 1953 to 1955, the Verbal Process opened in Taipeh, in Puy-en-Velay, in Sikkim and in Montauban, and forty witnesses were heard. They were unanimous in declaring the holiness of Fr Tornay and testified that his death had been brought about out of hatred for the Christian faith.

We learn from history how China occupied Tibet completely in 1959, how the Dalai-Lama went into exile in India, as the Red Flag flew over the Potala of Lhasa and of how six years later the country was given the status of "Autonomous Region".

Fr Savioz, who was last seen in 1949 at the tomb of Fr Maurice, revisited China in 1985 and 1987. The mission had been abandoned during the previous thirty years because the Fathers had been working in Formosa. When

103

"the Band of Four", who had been responsible for the communist regime after Mao, fell from power, Fr Savioz profited of the situation. Tensions between Formosa and the mainland, between nationalists and communists had eased, but because he showed too lively an interest in the Tibetan salt marshes, the local police were concerned and they confiscated all his films.

China and Tibet had changed considerably. The great misery had disappeared; good roads established communication between the plains and mountains; boldly built bridges spanned the rivers instead of the former perilous bamboo ropes. After 1980, a policy of appeasement was practised towards the Catholic religion and freedom of conscience, allowed previously in theory, now became a fact. The Office of Religious Affairs was established and recognised the Christian communities in Siao-Weisi, Tsechung, Bahang and Yerkalo. Churches were rebuilt for Christianity was still alive! But a large number of indigenous priests were needed to see to its needs.

In spite of this apparent greater openness, the movement of tourists and merchants was controlled with an iron fist. The Lamas had lost their power during the cultural revolution. Their system of slavery was abolished, many lamaseries were destroyed and traditional, cultural and architectural heritage was wiped out for good. Fr Savioz was quite astonished to see this. He noticed however that the country was trying to repair carefully, the destructive excesses to which it had been subjected.

He went to Tsechung, Weisi, Siao-Weis and finally to Atuntze where he wanted to pray at the tombs of the Servant of God and Doci, but they had disappeared. He found them about 125 kilometres above at Yerkalo, placed there by the Christians, faithful to their priest, their martyr and their holy one, as they waited for him to be declared their Saint if such was God's will.

* * *

No one can deny that the life and death of the Servant of God speak to us from a past with which we seem to have little affinity. It is difficult to imagine the hold and the demands of a Church which at that time held that salvation could not be found outside itself. It is also difficult to disregard the profound changes that have come about from the heroic times of the missions under Popes Benedict XV and Pius XI until the present day. In 1962, John XXIII under the impulse of the Holy Spirit opened Vatican II. This Council, in dialogue with the world, invited both clergy and laity to exercise their baptismal priesthood as "missionaries" and messengers of peace.

What still remains important is to discover what is the use for us today of the Beatification of the Servant of God on the feast of Pentecost 1993, and what will be its effect in Valais, in Switzerland and in China.

The spiritual qualities of Fr Tornay, which were perfected during the different circumstances of his brave and short life, namely his devotedness, his fidelity, his courage, his forgetfulness of self in his abandonment to God's grace, his commitment to the service of the most deprived, seemed less exceptional in the difficult times that have become our heritage. The merit of Fr Tornay was to have exercised these qualities up to the sacrifice of his life. He could have used the confused situation in Yunnan between 1946 and 1949, as a pretext to give up the mission of Yerkalo and to work elsewhere.

Our century, as it draws to an end, seems lost in individualism, indifference and confused values, from which the face of an "apostle" sometimes emerges. That is why today more than ever we need the bold witnesses, the martyrs and the saints. They were men who were truly part of our world, and they can be a refuge, a strength and an example to help us to rise above our egoism and inertia.

Without doubt, God may not ask of us the bloody sacrifice of our lives, as he did of the Servant of God, but we should imitate his courage and faith, his perseverance and self-denial so that the divine plan for each one of us may be accomplished according to each one's destiny.

Maurice Tornay is a guide who invites us to rekindle our conscience by approaching God who is love, and by becoming holy for the glory of the One who was his Absolute.

Notes

1   From a letter of St Thérèse of the Child Jesus to her sister (Celine, 26 April 1889.
2   *History of the Church*, Daniel-Rops, Ed. B. Grasset, vol XII, p. 203
3   *Land of Iron and Sky of Bronze*, Maurice Zermatten, p. 84
4   *Letters*, Father E. Jules. Dubernard FMP.
5   Cardinal Newman.
6   *Land of Iron and Sky of Bronze*, Maurice Zermatten, p. 175.
7   *Land of Iron and Sky of Bronze*, Maurice Zermatten, p. 191.
8   *Land of Iron and Sky of Bronze*, Maurice Zermatten, p. 213.
9   *Land of Iron and Sky of Bronze*, Maurice Zermatten, p. 244.

Bibliography

Letters and Writings: Father Maurice Tornay, Years 1925-1949.

A Martyr in Tibet, Robert Loup, ed. Great St Bernard Tibet, Fribourg, 2nd edition 1953.

Land of Iron and Sky of Bronze, the Passion of Fr Maurice Tornay, Maurice Zermatten, ed. Valmedia, Saviese 1988.

A Radiography of a Soul, the Witnesses speak, Andrea Ambrosi, Lawyer, Rome, 12 December 1989.

Summarium: Process of Information of the cause of Maurice Tornay, Carolus Snider, Lawyer. Revised, Mgr Amatus Petrus Frutaz, Under-Secretary, Rome, 1990

Relatio et Vota, Congressus Peculiaris super Martyrio, Vatican City, 12 December 1989.

The Mission of the Canons of the Great St Bernard in Tibet (1933-1952), Frederic Giroud, Fribourg, 1986. A Treatise presented for a Doctorate in Literature (Faculty of Literature, Fribourg University, Department of Modern and Contemporary History).

Thirty Years at the Gates of Forbidden Tibet, Francis Gore FMP.

Tibet, the Impossible Mission: Letters of Father E. Jules Dubernard, 864-1905, Le Sarment Fayard, 1990